Science Art + Drawing Games for Kids

35+ Fun Art Projects to Build Amazing Science Skills

KARYN TRIPP

CONTENTS

5 Introduction
6 What You'll Need
8 Key Science Concepts

1

Energy & Motion

16 Spin Art Machine
18 Spinning Helicopter Toy
20 Rainbow Gravity Spinner
22 Balancing Monsters
24 Flying Insect Automaton
28 Spinning Top Games
30 Monkey Climbing Toy
34 Paper Cup Zoetrope
36 Pantograph Drawing Machine
38 Paper Airplane Physics

2

Electricity & Magnetism

42 Paper Circuit Cards
44 Sound Wave Art
46 Magnet Pendulum Painting
48 Light-Up Pipe Cleaner Shapes
50 Magnet Mazes

3

Living Science

54 Atom Model Mobile
56 Homemade Natural Paints
58 Aquaponic Fish Tank
60 Plantable Seed Paper
64 Tiny Terrariums
66 Neuron Blow Paintings
68 DNA Punnett Square Insects

4

Chemical Reactions

72 Baking Soda & Vinegar Bubbly Painting
74 Homemade Exploding Paintballs
76 Cake Baking Experiment
78 Crystal Flower Garden
80 Color Mixing Bath Bombs
82 Making Plastic from Milk
84 Magic Color-Changing Lemonade
86 Oil & Water Painting

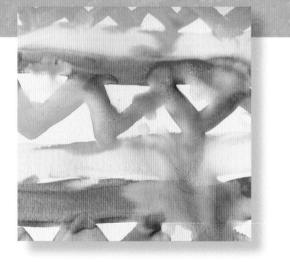

5

Color & Light

90 Glowing Highlighter Art
92 Solar Prints
94 Radial Chromatography
96 X-ray Nature Art
98 Shadow Drawings
100 Nebula Paintings
102 Seurat Pointillism
104 Marbled Paper
106 Homemade Kaleidoscope

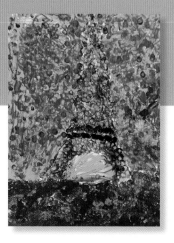

110 Acknowledgments
110 About the Author
111 Index

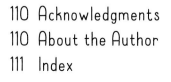

Introduction

Science is what makes the world go around. I have always loved science and was so excited to have the opportunity to create a science art book! I love that the world and all of its parts can be explained through biology, botany, astronomy, chemistry, and physics. And there is so much beauty in all of it.

My grandfather was an inventor. He was always building and creating things. I always remember him and the many stories of the things he made over the years. I got to take part in helping him build some of his inventions and it always stayed with me. I also watched my father build a car in our garage. Watching that process was inspiring to me. I know these influences in my life are a big part of what gave me my love for science.

I have always been awed and inspired by nature and the world around me. I love spring when the newness of life is bursting forth. I love watching plants grow to maturity and bear fruit. I am fascinated by rocks, shells, insects, and animals. I always want to know how and why things work, and this has led me to learn and study many of these things with my children over the years.

When I think of art and science together, Leonardo da Vinci comes to mind. He was someone who created both. I picture the David sculpture by the artist Michelangelo. Galileo, a famous scientist and astronomer, not only made new discoveries but created amazing art from the discoveries he made through his telescope. A famous botanist, Maria Sibylla Merian, created incredible art pieces based on plant life.

Often art and science are seen as opposites, but that could not be further from the truth! Artists use immense amounts of science in their creations and science is so full of art and beauty. They are virtually inseparable. Scientists keep notes and drawings of the things they learn and discover. Artists need to know chemistry and physics as they create their work. Many art techniques—such as photography, the making of paints, and the plaster used by many ancient artists—required a great amount of scientific knowledge to develop.

Science is one of the most fun subjects to explore and teach to kids. Exciting things can happen when you use principles of science to make art. You can create incredible art that may seem like magic in the process. Many of these activities are about the process as well as the product, so be sure to have fun in that process!

As you try out the projects in this book, I hope you'll be inspired to learn how and why they work. Behind each project is a science concept that you can study and learn more about. Science is truly awe inspiring and I hope you can develop your own love of science.

What You'll Need

These science-art activities will require a few supplies to make. Many of the supplies are common household items that you likely already have on hand. However, there are some specialty supplies that you'll need to acquire in advance. This supply list includes everything you'll need for the projects in this book. Stock up on all items or pick and choose certain projects and make sure you have all the required items to complete them. Once you have what you need, you can dive in and start creating and learning.

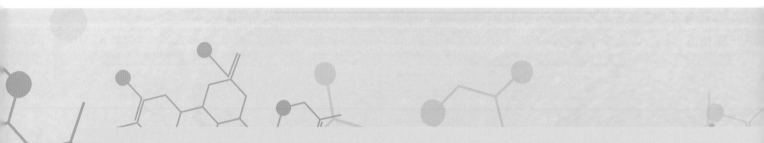

- AA batteries
- AA battery pack
- acrylic paint
- ammonia
- baking soda
- beads
- binder clips
- black light
- blender
- bluing
- buttons
- calcium chloride
- cardboard
- cardstock paper

- citric acid
- clay
- clear plastic cups
- coconut oil
- coin cell batteries
- computer
- conductive thread
- contact paper
- copper tape
- cornstarch
- cotton swabs
- craft foam sheets
- crayons
- dice

- dry erase markers
- duct tape
- eggs
- electrical tape
- embroidery thread
- Epsom salts
- eye droppers
- fabric squares
- felt squares
- filter paper
- fish
- flexible mirror
- flour
- flowers

- fruits and vegetables
- gears
- glass jar
- glue
- glue sticks
- google eyes
- graphite powder
- highlighter markers
- hobby motor
- hot glue gun
- insects
- iron filings
- LED lights
- lemonade

- liquid watercolors or food coloring
- magnets
- markers
- metal brads
- metal nut
- microscope
- paintbrushes
- paper
- paperclips
- parchment paper
- pebbles
- permanent markers

- pipe cleaners
- plants
- pom poms
- pots and pans
- printer
- prisms
- resin
- rubber bands
- rubbing alcohol
- ruler
- salt
- scissors

- seeds
- shaving cream
- silicone molds
- sodium alginate
- stove or microwave
- strainer
- sugar
- tape
- tempera paint
- toothpicks
- utility knife
- vanilla

- vegetable oil
- vinegar
- wall mounting tape
- watercolor paint
- wet erase markers
- wooden skewers
- yarn
- yogurt cups
- zipper close bags

Key Science Concepts

Throughout this book, you'll see "Science in Action" concepts for each project. These are terms that help explain the science behind the project and how it works. So, if you want to go deeper and learn more about it, this section can help you out.

Absorption: Taking in or soaking up liquid (or another substance).

Acid: A chemical substance that can be sour-tasting and can react with a base.

Aerodynamic: The way the air flies or glides around things.

Amphipathic: A substance that is both hydrophilic (mixes with water) and hydrophobic (repels water), such as soap.

Anatomy: The branch of science that studies the body structure of humans, animals, or other living things.

Animation: A series of photographs or drawings put together to create an illusion of movement.

Aquaponics: A form of food or plant production in which plants are grown in water that is also used to raise fish.

Astronomy: The branch of science that studies space, including planets, moons, stars, and galaxies.

Atom: The smallest basic unit of matter that forms chemical elements.

Base: In chemistry, a base is a substance that tastes bitter and reacts to acids.

Biology: The branch of science that studies living organisms, their behavior, origin, and make up.

Botany: The branch of science that studies plants, their structure, genetics, and classification.

Cams: Projecting rotating parts in a machine that are designed to help a machine move.

Capillary action: The ability of a liquid to flow in narrow spaces without assistance, even in opposition to gravity.

Carbon dioxide: A colorless gas that is formed by the breakdown of animal and plant matter. It is a vital part of the environment that is part of the air we exhale.

Casein: The protein found in milk and cheese.

Cells: The basic building block of all living things and the smallest structural unit of any organism. They provide structure for everything.

Center of gravity or Center of mass: Where the weight of an object is centered, the balance point of an object.

Centrifugal force: A force that moves a spinning object away from its starting point.

Chemical reaction: A process that changes or transforms a substance into something new.

Chemistry: The branch of science that deals with elements, atoms, molecules, their makeup, and behavior.

Chlorophyll: A green pigment present in all plants that helps convert sunlight into energy.

Chromatography: Separating a mixture by dissolving it in a liquid or gas as it moves through a stationary object such as filter paper.

Circuits: A closed path that allows electricity to flow from one point to another.

Color: The way a person sees light waves as they bounce off an object and reflect into their eyes.

Color spectrum: How colors are distributed when light shines through a prism.

Condensation: Water that has converted from a gas to a liquid and collected as droplets on a surface.

Conductivity: The rate at which heat or electricity passes through a material.

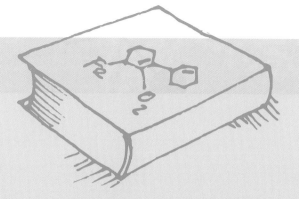

DNA: A molecule present in all living things that contains the instructions for how to develop and live.

Dominant trait: An inherited characteristic that will show up in the offspring if one of the parents contributes it.

Drag: Air resistance or friction that acts in the opposite direction of an object flying through the air.

Earth rotation: The spin or movement of the earth around its axis.

Ecosystem: A group of organisms living and interacting together with each other.

Electricity: The flow of charged particles or energy.

Electrons: Negatively charged particles in an atom.

Element: A pure substance made up of only one kind of atom that can't be broken down into simpler substances.

Endothermic reaction: A chemical reaction where heat is absorbed from its surroundings.

Engineering: The use of science and math principles to design and build things.

Evaporation: The process of a liquid turning to a gas.

Fluorescent: The ability of chemicals to give off light after absorbing it.

Force: A push or a pull on an object.

Fossils: Preserved remains of ancient plants or animals.

Friction: The resistance to motion as an object slides or moves across another object.

Gear: A rotating wheel with teeth around the edge that create motion in a machine when they turn.

Gravity: A force that pulls objects downward to earth.

Hydrophilic: A substance that mixes with or dissolves in water.

Hydrophobic: A substance that repels water or won't mix with it.

Immiscible: Substances that do not mix together, such as oil and water.

Kinetic energy: The energy of an object in motion.

Laws of motion: Three laws developed by Isaac Newton (1643–1727) that describe the motion of an object and the forces that act upon it.

Lever: A simple machine made by combining a beam or rod connected to a fixed point. When a force is applied to a lever, the load at the other end is lifted.

Lift: The upward force acting on an airplane or other flying object.

Machine: A mechanical device that uses power to apply force to an object, creating movement.

Magnetism: A force that attracts or repels objects caused by magnets and materials that contain iron or other metals.

Mechanical energy: The energy acquired when an object has done work such as motion or has a position above the earth with the potential to fall to the ground by way of gravity.

Mixture: A physical combination of two or more substances that are not chemically combined.

Molecules: A neutral group of two or more atoms held together by chemical bonds.

Nebula: A cloud of dust and gas in space between stars.

Nervous system: Cells and nerves that send signals between different parts of the body.

Neurons: Nerve cells in the brain that receive and send signals and commands to our muscles.

Neutrons: A neutrally charged particle in the nucleus, or center, of an atom.

Paleontology: The scientific study of the history of life on earth through analyzing plant and animal fossils.

Pendulum: A weighted object hung from a pivot or fixed point that swings freely.

Persistence of vision: An optical illusion where the brain retains an image for a short time after it is removed from sight. When seeing multiple still images in a short amount of time, the brain interprets them as motion.

pH indicator: Weak acids in natural dyes that change color when exposed to an acid or base, helping you determine which it is.

Photosensitive: An object that is sensitive to ultraviolet rays from the sun, causing a chemical change.

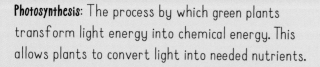

Photosynthesis: The process by which green plants transform light energy into chemical energy. This allows plants to convert light into needed nutrients.

Physics: A branch of science that studies matter, motion, and energy and how they interact.

Pigments: A water-soluble substance that gives an object color. They are typically used in dyes or paints.

Polarity: The separation of electrical charges, giving molecules a positive and negative end.

Polymer: A substance that has long chains of molecules.

Potential energy: Stored energy that is just waiting for a force to start it in motion.

Protons: A positively charged particle found in the nucleus of an atom.

Punnett square: A square diagram that is a grid of four boxes used to determine the possible genes of an offspring based on what traits the parents carry in their DNA.

Recessive trait: A weak trait that is carried in genes but not expressed unless both parents pass it on to their offspring.

Recycling: The process of collecting waste and converting it into material that can be made into new products.

Reflection: Light or sound waves changing direction and returning back to where it originated.

Shadows: A dark area where light is blocked from the rays of the sun by an object that is not see through.

Simple machines: Devices with few to no moving parts that are used to exert a force of motion. Examples include levers, wheels, pulleys, inclined planes, wedges, and screws.

Solution: A mixture of two substances in which one is dissolved into the other.

Sound waves: A movement or disturbance caused by energy traveling through air or water.

Space: The place beyond the earth's atmosphere that contains all of the planets, stars, and galaxies.

Technology: The branch of science focused on the application of scientific knowledge and the creation of new inventions.

Thrust: A force or push that moves an object in one direction, such as the force that moves an airplane through the air.

Torque: The measure of the force that causes an object to rotate.

Transpiration: The release of water from the leaves of plants into the air.

Wavelengths: The distance between two waves such as in sound, ultraviolet, electromagnetic, etc.

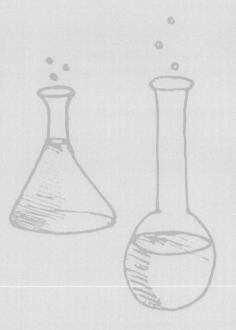

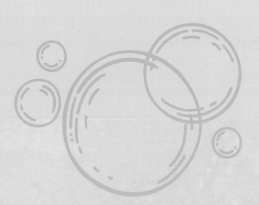

Energy & Motion

Physics is the branch of science that studies motion and energy. In this section of the book we are going to learn about force, energy, and motion. Kinetic energy is energy that is in motion. Potential energy is stored energy with the potential to be in motion, such as a toy that is wound up and about to be released or a bow that is pulled back and about to release an arrow.

When you use motion in art, you can create some amazing machines, toys, and games! In the projects here you'll be able to watch colors and images blend and move as they spin, and even make your own spinning and balancing toys! Sounds exciting, doesn't it? Let's dive in!

Spin Art Machine

When you combine art and physics you can make beautiful things! Learn how to build your own spin art machine that you can use with markers or paint. You'll learn a little about circuits and electricity as well as the science of motion, or physics.

Science in Action: *Centrifugal Force, Circuits, Electricity, Engineering, Physics*

What You'll Need

small hobby motor (3 V)

2 AA battery pack

electrical tape

small gear to fit on motor

wall mounting tape

cardboard box at least 12" (30 cm) in length on each side and at least 4" (10 cm) deep

utility knife

cardstock paper, cut into quarters (a few pieces for each person)

2 AA batteries

markers

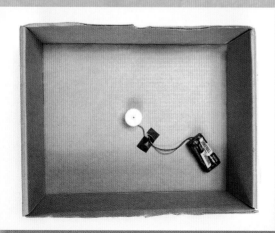

1 Begin by assembling your motor. Attach the wires from the motor to the battery pack, matching up the red and black wires. Secure the wires in place with a piece of electrical tape. Attach the gear to the top of the motor shaft.

2 Use a small piece of double-sided mounting tape on the bottom of the motor and attach it to the center of a cardboard box. Attach the battery pack in the same way. Tape down the wires to secure them to the box.

3 Use a utility knife to poke a small hole into the center of each quarter square of cardstock. Place mounting tape on the top of the gear and attach one piece of paper to the center by inserting the gear shaft through the hole.

4 Insert the batteries and watch it spin. Use markers to draw on the paper as it spins to create your art!

5 Pop out one battery to stop the motor and see what your finished art looks like.

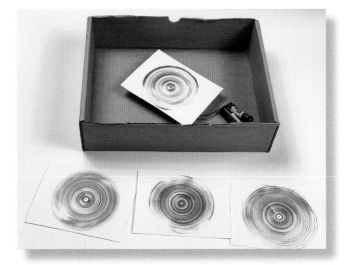

6 Add a new square of paper and try lots of different colors.

Spinning Helicopter Toy

This spinning helicopter is the perfect example of potential and kinetic energy. Potential energy is stored energy that can be released to create motion. When you release it, it then becomes kinetic energy. When you wind up this helicopter, it creates potential energy. Then when you release it and it spins; it is now kinetic energy! This helicopter does not fly, but it is still lots of fun to make and play with.

Science in Action: *Kinetic Energy, Potential Energy*

What You'll Need

small plastic cup with lid

utility knife

rubber band

toothpick

metal nut

straw

paper

scissors

hot glue gun

1 Use the utility knife to poke a small hole in the bottom of the cup and in the center of the lid.

2 Thread the rubber band through the hole in the bottom of the cup. Secure it in the bottom of the cup by threading a toothpick through the loop created by the rubber band.

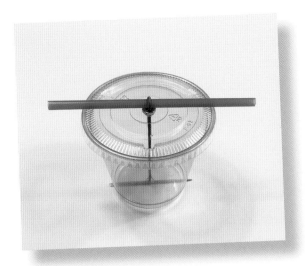

3 Pull the rubber band up and thread it through the lid of the cup. Next thread the rubber band through the center of the nut. To create the rotor for the helicopter, insert the straw through the rubber band loop, securing it between the rubber band and the lid.

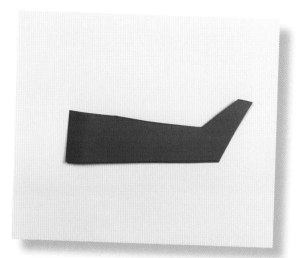

4 Cut a tail for your helicopter from paper. Fold a small section at the end and glue it onto the outside of the cup to make it look more like a helicopter. Decorate if desired!

5 To make the helicopter spin, twist the straw on the top several times and let it go. It will spin like the blades of a helicopter!

Rainbow Gravity Spinner

A scientist named Isaac Newton (1643–1727) discovered the laws of motion. The first law of motion states that an object will remain at rest or in uniform motion unless a force acts upon it. The third law of motion says that for every action there is an equal and opposite reaction. This spinner is propelled by rolling it between your hands and letting it fly. You create a force or action to make it spin and fly. Then the force of gravity lands the spinner on the ground. You decorate it in rainbow colors to create a beautiful swirl of mixed colors as it spins!

Science in Action: *Gravity, Laws of Motion*

1 Use a cup, bowl, or compass to trace a circle on a piece of cardstock. Using a ruler, divide the circle into six equal parts and color them the colors of the rainbow.

2 Cut out the circle. Cut between each color, stopping about three-quarters of the way to the center. Fold flaps downwards.

3 Straighten the paper clip. On one end, fold over a small section. Poke it through the center of your circle and tape down the folded section on the colored side.

4 Bend the other end of the paperclip a bit so it will insert into the straw and stay put. Cut your straw in half and insert the other end of the paper clip you just bent into it. This part will still be curved and should stay in place inside the straw.

5 To fly the toy, hold it between your palms so that the circle is facing up. Roll the straw quickly between your hands and let it go. It will spin and float, and you'll see the colors merge and blend as it flies!

Balancing Monsters

These fun balancing monsters are toys that can teach you about gravity. They will balance on a small stick because their weight is evenly distributed, creating a center of gravity. Gravity is the force that pulls things down to earth. The center of gravity is a special point where all of the weight is perfectly balanced. You may notice that if you don't set the monsters on the sticks evenly, they may lean to one side or the other.

Science in Action: *Center of Gravity, Gravity*

What You'll Need

large cork

2 12" (30 cm) wooden skewers or dowels

1 6" (15 cm) wooden skewer

¼ cup air dry clay

google eyes

pom poms

markers

hot glue gun

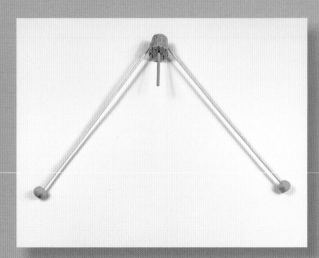

1 Insert the two long wooden skewers or dowels into the sides of the cork at a 45-degree angle. Make sure they are inserted in the same spot on each side for better balance.

2 Insert the small wooden skewer into the bottom center of the cork. Roll two small balls of clay and stick them to the ends of the two long wooden dowels.

3 Decorate your monsters as desired with google eyes, pom poms, and markers. Attach items using a hot glue gun. Draw stripes on the dowels and draw a mouth on the cork.

4 Balance the monster on the tip of your finger or the palm of your hand!

Flying Insect Automaton

An *automaton* is a moving mechanical device. They can be simple like the one we are going to make, or more complicated like a robot. The ancient Greeks created water-powered automata devices. Wind-up cuckoo clocks are also examples of automata. There are examples of mechanical devices in the records of King Solomon, Archimedes, and ancient China, as well as in Leonardo da Vinci's writings.

This fun project uses rotary movement, meaning it goes around in a circle. It's a mechanical toy that uses a crank and cams to move. A cam is a rotating piece that transfers energy or motion within a machine. When you spin the wooden stick, you spin the circle, or cam. It makes the other circle, called the cam follower, spin.

Have fun creating this mechanical device. Get creative with what you put on top too!

Science in Action: *Cams, Gears, Machines, Mechanical Energy*

What You'll Need

cardboard

compass

utility knife

scissors

clear plastic cup

2 wooden skewers 8–10" (20.5–25.5 cm) in length

colored craft foam or construction paper (optional)

hot glue gun

paper straw

pipe cleaners

1 Using a compass and a utility knife, cut two circles out of cardboard that are small enough to fit inside of your plastic cup. The ones pictured are about 2" (5 cm) in diameter. Cut two more smaller circles that are around ¾" (2 cm) in diameter.

2 Use the utility knife to poke three holes in your cup: one through the center of the bottom, a second through the side about halfway up, and a third directly across from the second.

3 Use scissors to cut off the sharp tips of the wooden skewers, taking off an extra inch (3 cm) to shorten them too.

4 If you wish, decorate your cardboard pieces with colored paper of craft foam. This is optional, but makes your automaton look more colorful! Poke holes through the center of all four cardboard circles.

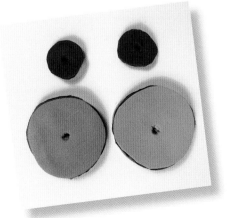

5 Attach one of the large circles to a wooden skewer with a hot glue gun. Insert the skewer just barely into the hole in the center and glue the top and bottom of the hole to secure it in place. This circle will go through the top of the cup.

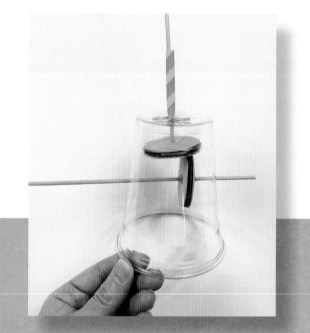

6 Cut off a 2–2¹⁄₃" (5–6 cm) piece from the straw. At one end of the piece cut a short slit and spread it apart. Glue the cut straw to the bottom of the cup just over the hole. From the inside of the cup, insert the skewer through the hole. The cardboard circle will be inside the cup.

7 Insert the second skewer through one hole in the side of the cup. Then inside the cup attach the second large cardboard circle to the skewer, lining it up with the top circle so it is off-centered. Next put the skewer through the hole on the other side of the cup. Do a test to make sure when you spin the wooden skewer it rotates the top circle. Secure this piece in place with hot glue. The bottom circle is the cam and the top circle is the cam follower.

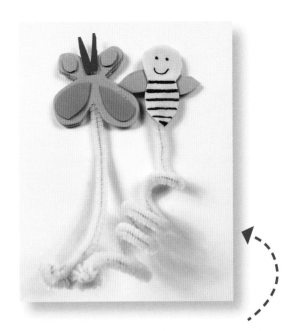

8 Now attach the two small circles to the skewer on the outside of the cup. Don't attach them to the cup, just the skewer. Push them in close to the cup and glue them in place. This keeps the skewers from sliding out as you spin them.

9 Create your insects or other creations with craft foam or colored paper, and glue them to the end of the pipe cleaners. Twist the pipe cleaners onto the top skewer. Glue a flower to the top of the skewer.

10 Decorate as desired! To move, spin the skewer to turn the cams. This will spin the insects on top.

Spinning Top Games

A spinning top is not just a child's toy, it's also a lesson in physics. Tops are amazing because when they spin they stand up and balance, but when they stop, they tip over. It's a rotational force called torque that causes the top to spin. The faster a top spins, the more likely it is to stay up. Play some games using a top. These games are all about the point when the top stops spinning.

Science in Action: *Force, Laws of Motion, Torque*

What You'll Need

ruler

scissors

cardboard

white paper

markers

glue stick

craft knife

wooden skewer

hot glue gun

buttons or other small items for game pieces

1 To make the top, measure and cut a 4" (10 cm) square from the cardboard and the white paper. Use a ruler to draw two corner-to-corner diagonal lines on the white paper. Color each section a different color. Glue the square of paper to the top of the cardboard square using a glue stick.

2 Poke a small hole in the center of the top using scissors or a craft knife. Cut the wooden skewer down to about 3–4" (7.5–10 cm) in length. Insert the skewer through the hole in the center of the cardboard. The point of the skewer should be on the bottom side. Center the cardboard on the skewer, leaving about 2" (5 cm) of length at the top and the bottom. On the bottom side, use a dab of hot glue to secure the skewer in place.

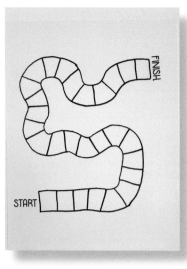

3 On a separate piece of paper, draw a game board. You can make it any design or shape you want.

4 Color in the squares using the same four colors you used on the top. To play this game, spin the top and allow it to fall to one side. Move the game piece to the colored space on which the top landed.

5 For a second game option, make four columns marked with the four colors used on the top. Each player chooses a color to "bet" on. Spin the top a chosen number of times and add a tally mark in the column of the color where it lands. The player who chose the color with the most tallies wins!

Monkey Climbing Toy

The monkey climbing toy works through something called friction. Friction is a resisting force that occurs between two objects that are sliding across each other. This force works in the opposite direction from how the object is moving or trying to move.

When you make your monkey climbing toy, you'll create friction or traction between the arms. Think about the bottom of a pair of shoes when you climb a rocky hill. If your shoes have good traction, it's easier to climb. But if your shoes have slippery soles, you'll just slide back down! This friction is what allows the monkey to climb up the vine!

Science in Action: *Force, Friction*

What You'll Need

cardboard

pencil

utility knife

3 toothpicks

¾" (2 cm) metal brad

hot glue gun

felt or craft foam

scissors

3' (92 cm) length of yarn

pipe cleaner

markers

small rubber band

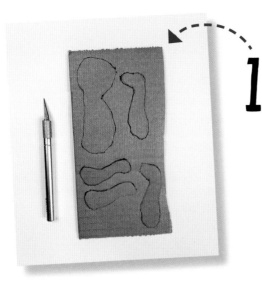

1 On the cardboard, draw the shapes for the body of your monkey (or other design you choose). You'll need a body, two matching arms, and two matching legs. Use a utility knife to cut out the pieces.

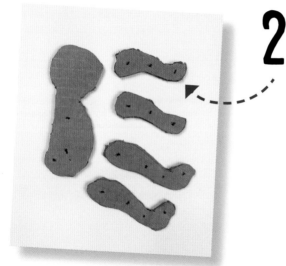

2 Use a toothpick to poke three holes in the arms and four holes in the legs, making sure the holes on each arm and leg match up with each other. Then poke two holes through the body where you'll attach the arms and legs.

3 Cut three toothpicks in half and insert them through the holes going through both legs. Use a metal brad to attach the legs to the body, pushing the brad through all three layers of cardboard.

4 Use a dab of hot glue to secure the toothpicks in place on the front and the back of the legs.

5 Before attaching the arms, cut the felt or craft foam into 4½" (1.3 cm) squares. Use glue to attach a piece to the inner sides of each arm between the first and second holes. This will create the friction needed for the toy to climb up the string.

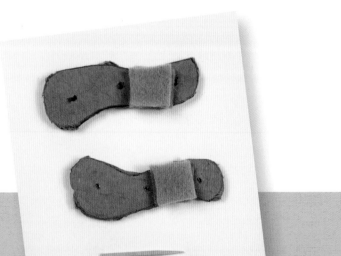

6 Place the yarn between the two arms, running through the center of the felt pieces that were attached to the arms in the previous step. Thread the yarn down through the legs, looping under the third toothpick then up and over the second toothpick.

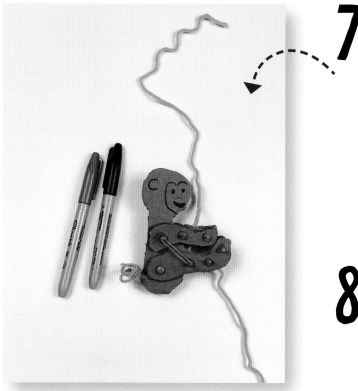

7 Attach the arms by inserting the toothpicks into each of the three holes. Secure each one with hot glue on the front and back. Loop the rubber band on the left side of the toothpicks for the arms and the legs to connect them. This adds more friction, making it easier for the monkey to climb.

8 Draw a face on your monkey. Make another small hole for the monkey's tail. Use half of a pipe cleaner and twist it into the hole to secure it. Curl it around your finger to make it twisty.

9 Now it's play time! To make the monkey climb the vine, hold both ends of the yarn and pull on the top one. The monkey will move up the yarn to the top. Slide it down to try it again!

Paper Cup Zoetrope

What's a zoetrope? These were first created in the 1800s before we had film to create animation. The word *zoetrope* comes from Greek root words meaning "wheel of life." A zoetrope is a circular device with slits around the sides. You'll insert drawings inside of it and spin it around. As you spin it your eyes and your brain will see the images through the slits and perceive motion, filling in the missing spaces. This is a type of optical illusion called persistence of vision. Early cartoons were made in a similar way with a series of hand drawn pictures put together to create motion.

What You'll Need

dark colored paper cup (*if you don't have a dark-colored paper cup, paint the outside with black acrylic paint*)

ruler

2 pieces of white paper

scissors

pencil or wooden dowel

markers

tape or glue

Science in Action: *Animation, Persistence of Vision*

1 Prepare your supplies. Paint the cup if needed to create contrast. Cut small slits around the top of the cup, spacing each slit is about 1" (2.5 cm) apart and cutting them about 1½" (4 cm) deep.

2 Measure the distance from the bottom of the slits to the bottom of the cup. Cut the paper into strips that are the same width as that measurement and about an inch (2.5 cm) longer than the circumference of the inside of the cup. On your paper strips, draw several pictures or patterns. Leave ½" (1 cm) blank on both ends of the strips for the paper to overlap. Remember that these patterns should look like they are in motion when you spin the zoetrope. Some ideas include a fish jumping in and out of the water, a pattern of moving lines, dancing or running stick figures, or any other ideas you can come up with! Make as many different animation strips as you would like.

3 Poke a hole in the bottom of the cup and insert a pencil or wooden dowel. Add a dab of hot glue or some tape to secure the dowel and keep it from wobbling.

4 Insert your picture strips into the cup. The overlapping sections will keep the paper in place, so there's no need to secure it.

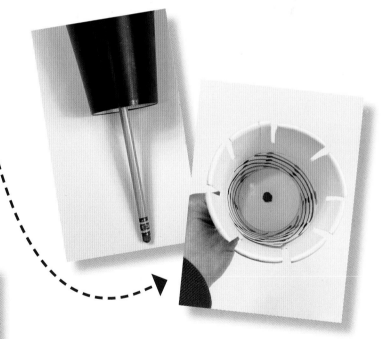

5 Spin your zoetrope at your eye level while looking through the slits on the side at the pictures as they move. Create more pictures on additional strips of paper.

Pantograph Drawing Machine

A *pantograph* is a simple machine that was used by Greeks in ancient times to trace images. There are two pencils that draw identical images, but in different sizes. The pantograph uses a lever to move in and out or back and forth as you draw with it. Engineers and artists use pantographs to reduce or enlarge their drawings. Now you can create your own simple version and see how it works. It's both entertaining and surprising to watch the second pen as it draws the same image!

What You'll Need

cardboard

utility knife

metal brads

paper

markers or colored pencils

scissors

tape

Science in Action: *Levers, Simple Machines*

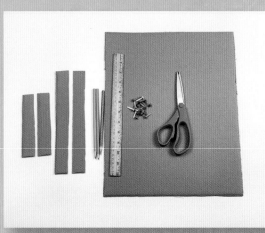

1 Use a utility knife to cut four strips of cardboard about 1" (2.5 cm) wide. Cut two of the pieces 10" (25.5 cm) long and two of the pieces 6" (15 cm) long. You'll also need a large piece of cardboard for the base. The piece we used was 16 x 14" (40.5 x 35.5 cm).

2 Connect the two long pieces with a metal brad. Make the holes for the brad with a pair of scissors or a utility knife.

3 In the center of each of the long pieces, attach one of the smaller pieces using metal brads. Pull the unattached ends of the smaller pieces together and overlap them. Use scissors to poke a hole through both pieces that's big enough to hold a pencil or marker.

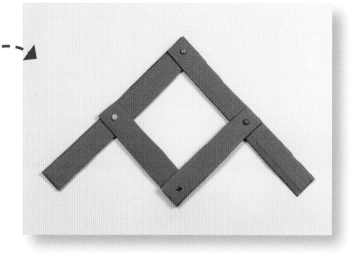

4 Poke holes at the bottom of each of the long pieces. The one on the right will hold a pencil or marker. The one on the left will connect with a metal brad to the cardboard base. Tape a large piece of paper over the square cardboard base. Connect the pantograph to the bottom left corner of the base with a metal brad.

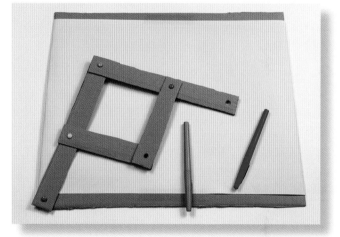

5 Insert markers or pencils through the holes on the other two ends. Use the pencil attached to the shorter pieces to draw a picture on the large piece of paper covering the base. As you draw, watch as the marker on the left will draw the same image, but larger!

Paper Airplane Physics

Have you ever thought about how much science goes into the flying of a paper airplane? There are four forces that help an airplane to fly: thrust, lift, drag, and gravity. Thrust is the forward movement you give it when you throw it. Lift happens when air gets under the plane and pushes it upward. Drag is the force of resistance that acts on the plane as it goes through the air. Gravity is the force that pulls it down. The goal is to defy gravity as much as possible to increase the flight time. That's where your airplane design comes in! The type of design you use will determine how high and how far it will fly.

Design a few different types of paper airplanes by folding them in different ways. I'll show you two below. Test them out and see which one is the most aerodynamic.

Science in Action: *Aerodynamic, Drag, Gravity, Lift, Thrust*

What You'll Need

several pieces of paper

ruler

pencil

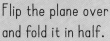

Red Plane

1 Fold your paper in half with the long sides meeting up and open it again. Fold the two top corners of the short side into the center of the paper.

2 Fold the top edges in to the center again.

3 Flip the plane over and fold it in half.

4 Finish by folding each of the wings down.

Blue Plane

1 Fold the paper in half with the short sides meeting up and unfold it.

2 Then follow steps 1 through 3 from the red plane instructions.

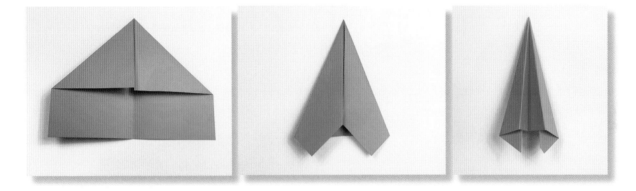

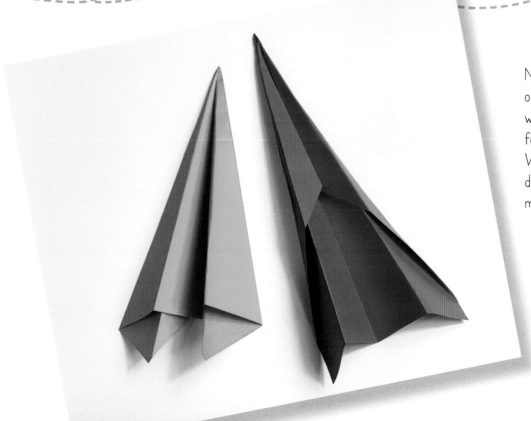

Now test out each of the planes. See which plane flies the farthest most often. What aspects of the design do you think makes it fly best?

Electricity & Magnetism

In this chapter, you'll learn how magnets and electricity work, then be amazed at the exciting projects you can create with this new knowledge. Play with and make art magnets and electricity, make light-up cards, paint and sew with electricity, make art with your voice, and even paint with magnets! These are a few of the interesting projects you get to try out in this chapter. Tap into your creativity to put your own unique spin on each of these science art projects.

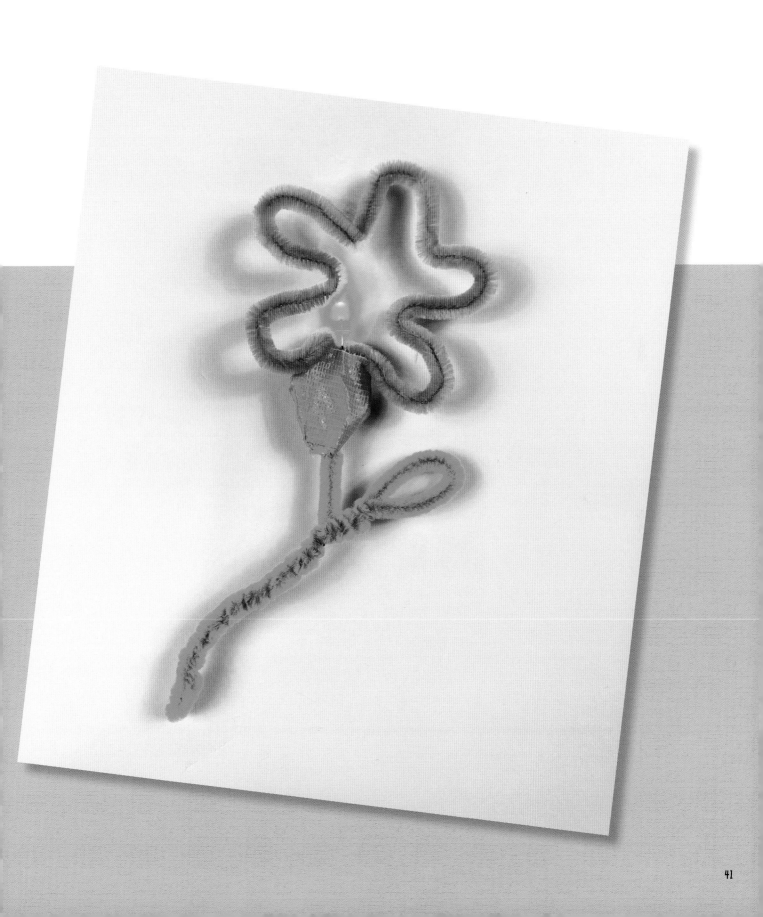

Paper Circuit Cards

In this project you can make extra special light-up cards for your friends and family! Dream up any design you like for these cards, then light them up! There are many ways to make electrical circuits, and this is one of the easiest. The circuits on these cards are made on paper with conductive copper tape, a small light, and a round battery. They're fun and easy to make, and once you know how, you'll want to make them for everyone!

Science in Action: *Circuits, Conductivity, Electricity*

What You'll Need

- paper
- hole punch
- markers
- copper tape
- scissors
- glue stick
- LED lights
- coin cell battery
- small binder clip

1 Decide on the design of your card. Fold a blank piece of paper in half. On the front half create your card design by drawing a picture and deciding where you want your light to be.

2 Use a hole punch to punch a hole in the front of the card in the spot where you want the light.

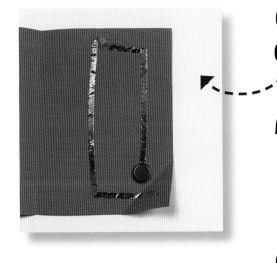

3 Open up the card. On the inside, fold the bottom corner in. Using the copper tape, make a line starting from the fold going straight up the paper to the place where your light will be.

4 Start a second line of copper tape a short distance away that extends up to the other side of the light. These two lines can't cross but should be close enough together that the pins of the light will touch both of them when they are bent outwards.

5 One line will be the positive line and one line will be the negative line. The pins on the lights are two different lengths. The longer one is the positive side, and the shorter one is the negative side. Fold the pins out so they touch each line and cover the top with tape to secure the light. Make sure the light fits into the hole in the front of the card as well.

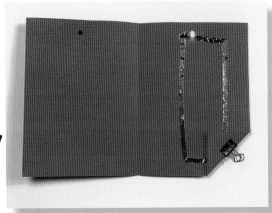

6 To attach the battery, place it so the positive side touches the same line of copper tape that's paired with the long end of the pin. Fold over the corner so the battery touches both copper tape lines and secure it with a small binder clip. If the light does not light up, make sure your battery is facing the right direction and that there are no breaks in the tape.

7 Write in your card and finish decorating to make it just right!

Sound Wave Art

Did you know that sound travels in waves, just like the waves you see in an ocean or lake? You just can't see them. A sound wave is a vibration or disturbance in the air made from sounds. The air moves back and forth as the sound is transmitted.

This project combines art and technology to make a picture of the sound waves created by your voice. For this project, you'll need access to a computer with audio recording software. There are many free audio software programs available. Some computers include them already.

Science in Action: *Sound Waves, Technology, Wavelengths*

What You'll Need

scissors or paper cutter

colored paper and white paper

glue stick

computer with audio recording software or a phone with a voice memo application

printer

1 Use recording software to record yourself saying a short phrase (2 to 3 words). In the one pictured, we said "I love you." Take a screenshot of the sound wave created from your recorded voice. Then edit the image, increasing the size to fill the page. Print the image.

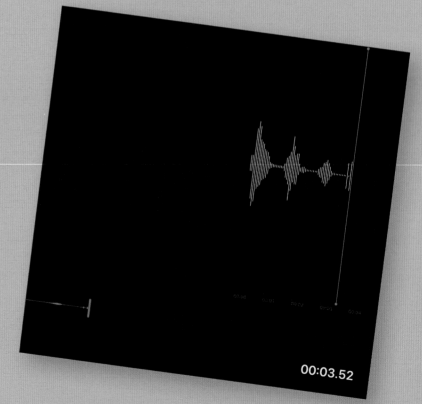

00:03.52

2 Cut colored papers into thin strips using a paper cutter or a pair of scissors.

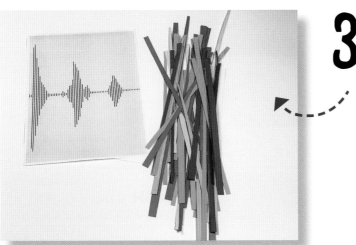

3 Looking at the sound wave, cut your strips of paper into lengths that approximately match the wave. They don't have to be exact. Also, you won't be able to fit the same number of strips on your paper that are contained in your sound wave, since the paper strips will be wider than the lines in your printout.

4 Glue your strips onto a white piece of paper with a glue stick, beginning with the center of your design and working outward to fit the entire design on the page.

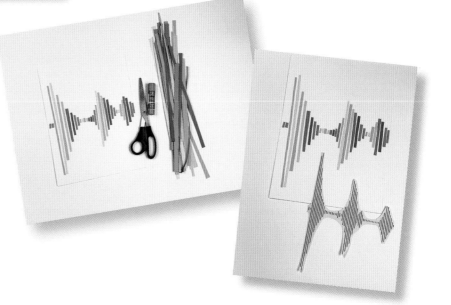

Magnet Pendulum Painting

A pendulum is a swinging object that hangs from a string or rod. The weight of the object, the length of the string, and forces of gravity all play into how fast it will swing. Potential and kinetic energy keep it moving.

This project will take a little bit of trial and error to get it working just right. But science is often that way! Magnets are so fun to play with and test out. Get this pendulum swinging so you can make a work of art.

What You'll Need

broomstick or other long pole

2 chairs or stools

magnet wand

string or yarn

small paintbrush

strong magnets

paint

large white paper

1 Begin by building your pendulum. Place a broom stick across two chairs or stools. Attach a magnet wand to a piece of string, and then tie the other end of the string to the broomstick. If you don't have a magnet wand, you can make your own using the instructions in the magnet maze project on page 50, but you'll want this one to have a magnet on both sides of the stick. Hang the wand at a length that leaves a little bit of clearance at the bottom.

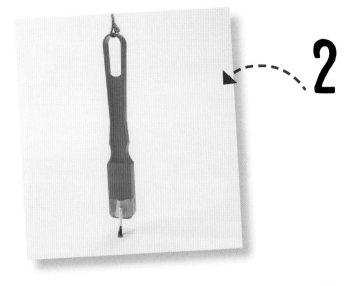

2 Tape a small paintbrush to the bottom of the magnet wand, giving it enough length to brush the paper you place underneath. The brush needs to be as lightweight as possible so it can swing freely. We removed the tip of the brush from the handle to lighten it.

3 Place a large piece of paper underneath the pendulum. Add more magnets as needed to control the movement of the magnet wand. Try placing magnets on the paper in a ring around the pendulum so it swings, or hold other magnets close to the wand to cause it to move and swing. If you place the magnets in a ring around the center magnet wand, try testing it out without the brush first to see what motions work best. If you flip the magnets in different directions, you'll get different results.

4 Now dip your brush in the paint and see what pictures it creates as you make the magnets swing!

Light-Up Pipe Cleaner Shapes

Pipe cleaners are fun to use in art projects, but did you know you can use them in science projects, too? This project combines both by using the metal wire in the center of the pipe cleaner to conduct electricity. Just connect a light and a battery and magic happens! What light-up creations can you make with your pipe cleaners? Start with a simple shape like a circle or a star to get the hang of it.

Science in Action: *Circuits, Electricity*

What You'll Need

dark colored paper cup

pipe cleaners *(for the best electrical connection, peel the fuzz off the ends of the pipe cleaners so the wire can connect to the battery and lights)*

LED pin lights

coin cell batteries

duct tape

small 12" (30 cm) wooden dowel

beads

1 Using two pipe cleaners or cutting one in half, connect the ends of each one to one of the pins of the LED light. The pins on the end of the light have different lengths. The longer one should connect to the positive side of your battery, and the shorter one should connect to the negative side of the battery.

2 Now bring the other pipe cleaner ends to the battery with the positive one touching the positive side and the negative one touching the negative side. Your light should turn on. Remember the two pipe cleaners can't touch each other or the light won't work. Tape around the battery and wires to secure it in place.

3 Now that you understand the basic idea of how it works, make your own light-up creations! To make the star wand, form a star out of pipe cleaners and attach the light at the top of the star and the battery at the bottom. Tape a wooden dowel to the battery to make the wand.

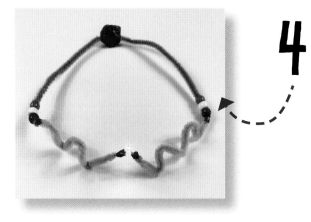

4 To make the crown, use one pipe cleaner to shape the front, attaching the light in the front center and the battery in back of it. Use two pipe cleaners to make it large enough to fit around your head. When using more than one pipe cleaner, peel the fuzz off the ends of each one to get a better connection. Add beads and tape at the connection points to secure and decorate.

5 For the flower, use two colored pipe cleaners, one for the flower and one for the stem.

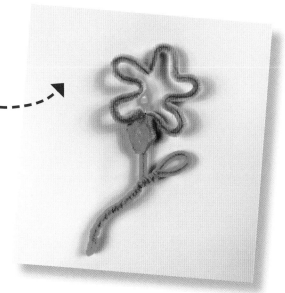

Magnet Mazes

Magnet mazes are an enjoyable way to play with magnets and learn how to move them around. You can also play with different items to test if they are magnetic or not. Design your own styles of mazes and race your friends and family to see who can do the mazes the fastest.

Science in Action: *Magnetism, Polarity*

What You'll Need

magnet wand, or large craft stick

paper

small magnets

markers

hot glue

small metal objects

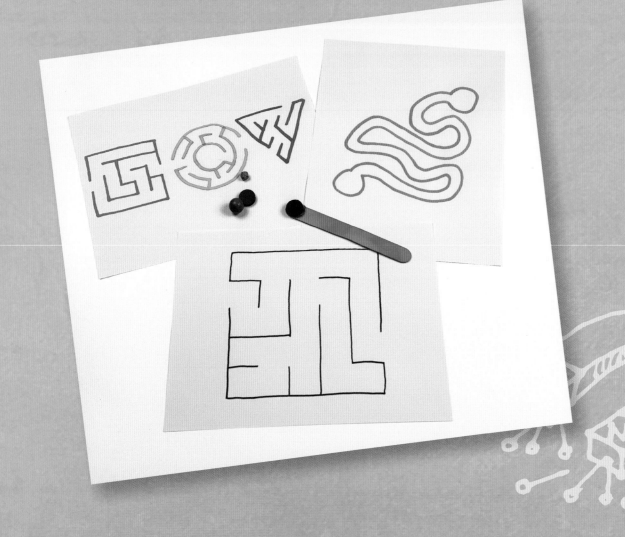

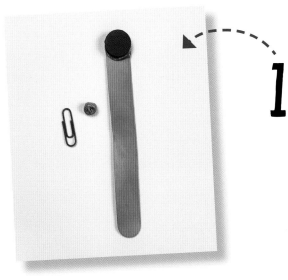

1 If you don't have a magnet wand, make your own using a large craft stick, a magnet, and some strong glue. We used a hot glue gun. Simply glue the magnet to the end of the craft stick.

2 Draw or print out several different styles of mazes.

3 Place small metal objects or another small magnet on the top of the paper maze with the magnet wand underneath the paper. Maneuver the object through the maze; the magnet underneath will follow along.

Living Science

Science is alive and it is exciting! Biology is the study of living organisms. In this chapter we'll explore all kinds of living things such as DNA, atoms and molecules, plants, and even animals! But more than just learning, you'll be creating art in the process!

Learn to preserve some plants and insects and grow some new living things. Explore the neurons in the brain. Make paint out of fruits, vegetables, and spices, and make models of atoms and elements. If you ever thought science was not cool, think again!

Atom Model Mobile

The world is made up of atoms, which are the basic units of matter. The elements on the periodic table are made of all one type of atom. With this project you'll build models of atoms and make them into beautiful hanging pieces of art! The models pictured here are two types of elements from the periodic table: Oxygen and Neon. Use this fun activity to learn more about what atoms are and how they make up the whole world. Create a model of your favorite element!

What You'll Need

images of different atoms

pipe cleaners or wire

beads

string

scissors

Science in Action: Atoms, Chemistry, Electrons, Elements, Molecules, Neutrons, Protons

1 Look up different atoms and elements to learn about the different parts and how they look. Choose one that you would like to build.

2 Begin by building the nucleus. This is the center of the atom, made up of protons and neutrons. You'll need to learn about the atom you're building to know how many protons and neutrons you'll need in your nucleus. For example, the element oxygen pictured has eight of each. Thread a pipe cleaner with beads to represent them.

3 Twist the pipe cleaner up into a ball and trim off any extra wire.

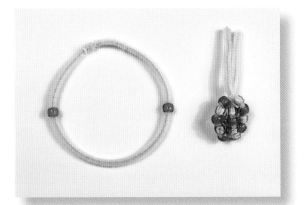

4 The electrons orbit around the nucleus. Build your first orbit by adding the correct number of electrons (beads) to your pipe cleaner. For oxygen, there are two electrons in the first orbit. Twist the pipe cleaner into a circle.

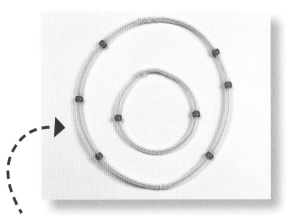

5 Build your second, and third orbit if needed, in the same way. Oxygen has six electrons in the second orbit.

6 Tie each of the parts together with string. Then tie a long string at the top and hang your mobile.

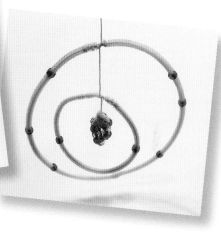

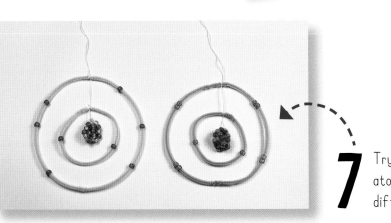

7 Try making different atoms and elements with different colors!

Homemade Natural Paints

Before we had paints with vibrant colors that you can buy at your local store, people made their own using items from nature! Pigments are what create the vibrant colors in plants. Plant pigments include: Chlorophyll (green), Carotenoids (orange, red, yellow, pink), and Flavonoids (yellow, red, blue, purple). Make your own homemade paints in this project with natural items from your fridge or yard. The pigments used in this project come from various plants.

Science in Action: *Biology, Chlorophyll, Photosynthesis, Pigments*

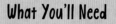

What You'll Need

- spinach
- carrots
- beets
- turmeric
- paprika
- flower petals
- berries
- grass
- onion skins
- blender or food processor
- stove or microwave
- fine strainer
- paint brushes
- watercolor paper

1 Collect brightly colored natural materials or objects for use in making your paints. Test out the ones we used (see What You'll Need, above) or try your own!

2 Boil each item individually with water on the stove or in a microwave until softened and color has been released into the water. Blend your items with the cooking water in a food processor or blender.

3 Pour the mixture through a fine metal strainer or sieve to get rid of pulp or chunks.

4 Pour the remaining liquid into small bowls. Test out your paints to see what the colors look like on paper.

5 Paint pictures using your new paints!

Aquaponic Fish Tank

Aquaponics is a system of growing that combines raising aquatic animals with growing plants in water. The plants and animals provide the nutrients to help each other thrive. The plants absorb nutrients from the fish waste and the bacteria from the plant roots are good for the fish. Aquaponics has been used for thousands of years in many cultures around the world, including the Aztecs and the Chinese. Create your own aquaponics system by growing a plant in the same container where you raise a pet fish!

Science in Action: *Aquaponics, Biology*

What You'll Need

utility knife

empty yogurt cup that fits into the top of the jar

glass jar

pebbles or marbles

purified water

wheat, grass, or other seeds

fish (Goldfish or Beta fish recommended)

1 To make your growing container, use a utility knife to cut slits into the sides and poke a few holes in the bottom of the yogurt container. This will allow water to nurture the plants and provide a place for the roots to grow down.

2 Decorate the bottom of the glass jar with rocks or pebbles and fill it with purified water, leaving a couple of inches at the top for the yogurt cup.

3 Fill the yogurt cup with pebbles or stones and sprinkle a few seeds on the top. Insert the cup into the jar filled with water.

4 You can start the plant before adding the fish or you can add the fish right away. The grass grows quite quickly and should sprout within a few days. When you need to feed your fish or clean the water, just lift up the plant and feed or clean as needed.

5 Place in a sunny spot where the plant and the fish receive lots of light.

Plantable Seed Paper

Paper, as you might know, is made from trees. Wood is ground into chips, then boiled down to make a pulp which is pressed flat to make paper. The cells in the wood dissolve and stick together when the paper is dry. This project allows you to recycle some already made paper into a new paper. And guess what? This paper will grow if you plant it! Use the paper you make to create cards for friends and family.

Science in Action: *Botany, Recycling*

What You'll Need

shredded recycled paper

dish bin or large bowl

blender or food processor

large, rimmed cookie sheet

muslin fabric, cheesecloth, or other thin fabric

large spoon

small seeds, such as wildflower seeds

dried flower petals

rolling pin

dish towels

cutting board or other hard surface

paints or other colored papers to decorate

1 Shred papers you no longer need. This is a great way to recycle mail, newspapers, or school papers. If you don't have a paper shredder, cut or tear the paper into small pieces.

2 Place the pieces in a dish bin or large bowl and cover with water. The quantities don't matter, just be sure all the paper is covered. Soak the paper for a few hours to soften it. Or, to speed up the process, pour hot water over the paper.

3 Combine the paper and water mixture in a blender or food processor. Try to get it as smooth as possible.

4 Cover a large, rimmed cookie sheet with a piece of muslin fabric, cheesecloth, or other thin fabric. Scoop or pour some of the mixture onto the fabric. Spread it flat with a spoon. Sprinkle seeds and flower petals over the top and use the spoon to press them down into the paper mixture.

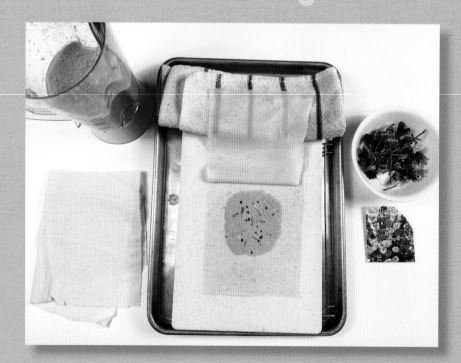

5 Cover the mixture with another piece of fabric and a towel. Roll over it with a rolling pin to squeeze out excess water.

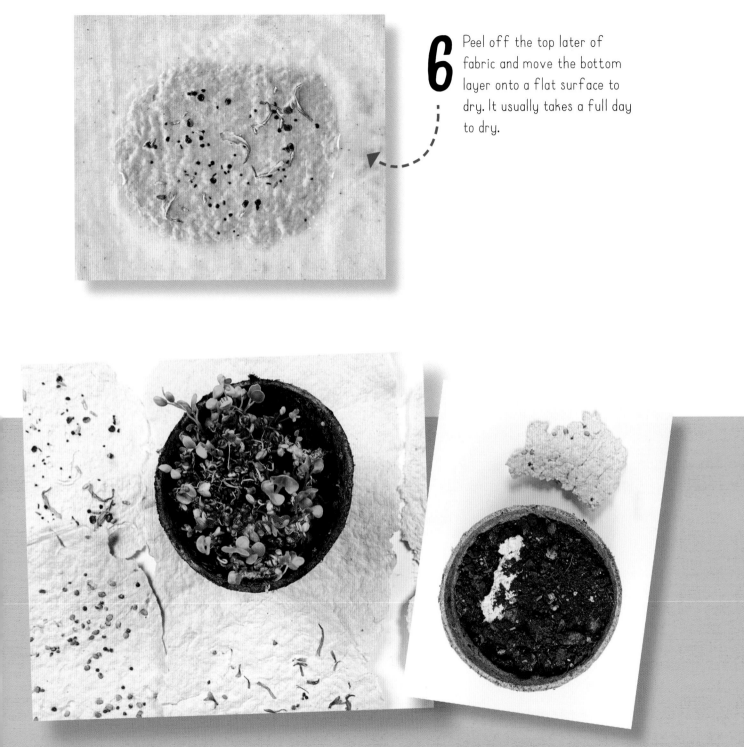

6 Peel off the top later of fabric and move the bottom layer onto a flat surface to dry. It usually takes a full day to dry.

7 Once the paper is dry, paint messages, attach it to another piece of colored paper, or decorate as desired. These make lovely cards for friends and family.

8 The paper can then be planted and sprouted!

Tiny Terrariums

A terrarium is a sealed container containing a miniature garden inside. It's usually an ecosystem that can almost entirely sustain itself by self-watering through transpiration and condensation. These tiny terrariums can be made into necklaces or displayed on a shelf or table.

Science in Action: *Botany, Condensation, Ecosystem, Transpiration*

What You'll Need

moss, small plants, and other nature objects

tiny glass vials with cork stoppers or domes with wooden base

tweezers

eye screw (optional)

necklace or string if desired

1 Collect moss, plants, and other tiny natural objects to display in your terrarium. Moss works well in terrariums because it is low maintenance, doesn't need much light, and likes a lot of moisture.

2 Fill the vials with plants and other nature objects. Since these are so small, use tweezers to insert and arrange them.

3 The domed terrarium can be filled by inserting plants into the dome or on the base. To water, just lift the top and add a tiny drop or mist of water.

4 If you want to make a necklace with your tiny terrarium, screw an eye screw into the top of the cork and hang it on a string or necklace. The cork can be removed to add a drop of water as needed and keep your plants alive.

Neuron Blow Paintings

Neurons are nerve cells in the nervous system, and they make up part of the brain. They are an important part of our brain because they send and receive signals and information throughout our body. Neurons have lots of little extensions called dendrites that look sort of like branches. This project was inspired by the work of Santiago Ramón y Cajal (1852–1934), a Spanish neuroscientist who studied the central nervous system extensively. He created many incredible drawings of neurons and cells. He was awarded a Nobel Prize for his work and discoveries on the nervous system. This project allows you to create beautiful artwork that looks like neurons. It's made by blowing paint through a straw. Sound like fun? Give it a try!

What You'll Need

watercolor paints, such as liquid watercolors

watercolor paper

straws

Science in Action: *Cells, Nervous System, Neurons*

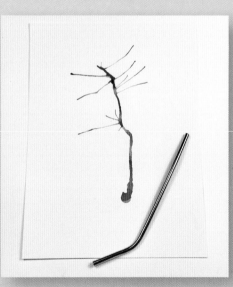

1 Add one or two small drops of color onto your paper. It works best to do one or two drops at a time, otherwise, they soak into the paper and don't move around.

2 Use a straw to blow the paint around the paper. Turn the paper as you move the paints around.

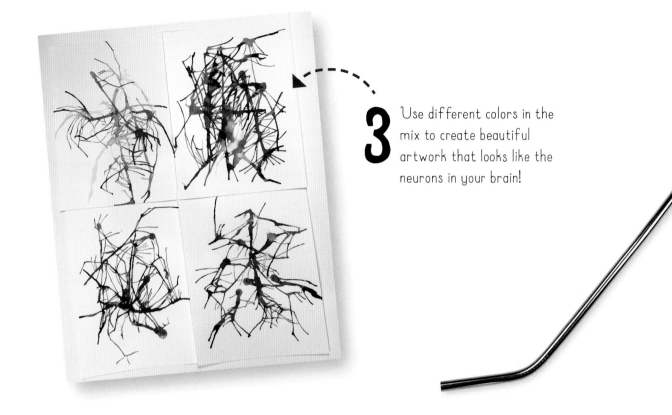

3 Use different colors in the mix to create beautiful artwork that looks like the neurons in your brain!

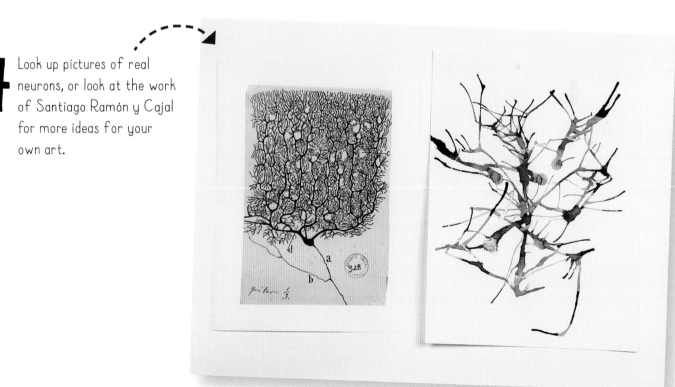

4 Look up pictures of real neurons, or look at the work of Santiago Ramón y Cajal for more ideas for your own art.

DNA Punnett Square Insects

DNA is the material in your body that carries all of the information about how your body looks and functions. We each have unique DNA that is given to us by our parents. A scientist named Reginald Punnett (1875–1967) developed a square diagram with a grid of four boxes that is used to depict all the possible combinations of genes we can receive from our parents. With this project, you'll use a simplified version of this to create your own insects. This is a fun way to get an idea of how DNA works!

Science in Action: *Dominant Trait, DNA, Recessive Trait, Punnett Square*

What You'll Need

paper

pencil

sheet protector or laminator

markers, colored pencils, or crayons

paper clip

metal brad

pair of dice

dry erase marker

1 Make a chart and decide on the traits of your insects. You can use the ones in the chart provided or come up with your own. Assign each trait a letter with the dominant trait assigned the capital letter and the recessive trait assigned the lowercase letter.

TRAIT	DOMINANT	RECESSIVE
A- Body Color	A- Any Color	a- Red
B- Body Length	B- Long	b- Short
C- Body Width	C- Fat	c- Skinny
D- Eye Size	D- Large	d- Small
E- Antennae Shape	E- Straight	e- Curly
F- Wing Shape	F- Wide	f- Narrow
G- Leg Length	G- Short	g- Long
H- Design	H- Spots	h- Stripes
I- Defense	I- Stinger	i- Claws

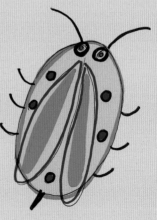

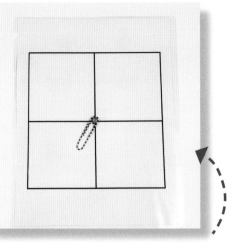

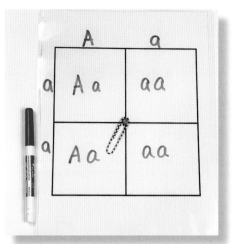

2 Draw or print a Punnett Square. This is just a square divided into four equal parts. Use markers or crayons to make it colorful. Laminate the paper or slide it into a sheet protector. This square will also be a game spinner. Poke a small hole in the center of the square and put a metal brad through the hole. Insert a large paper clip between the paper and the brad.

3 For each trait you'll roll the dice twice to choose the parent traits for the Punnett Square. Numbers 1–3 represent the dominant traits and numbers 4–6 represent the recessive traits. For example, if you're choosing the traits for the Body Color and the first roll is a 1 and a 4, you'll write capital A on top of the first box and lowercase a on top of the second box. When you roll again for the letters on the side you roll a 5 and a 6, you write two lowercase a's along the side squares.

4 Fill in the Punnett Square using the traits rolled. Use a dry erase marker so you can wipe and re-use the Punnett Square for a new game. Spin the spinner to determine which trait your bug will have. Any square with a capital A will be dominant, giving you a bug of any color.

5 Continue spinning to determine each trait. Draw your bug as you go or draw the entire bug at the end with all the traits you rolled. Play with a friend and see how your bugs differ!

4 Chemical Reactions

If you like the kind of science that is full of surprises, chemical reactions, and interactions, this section is for you! In this chapter you'll paint with bubbles, grow crystal flowers, make your own plastic, and make food that is both tasty and science inspired! My personal favorite is the homemade paintballs. You have got to try them.

All of these activities have some sort of change or reaction that takes place as you create them. They are fun to make and interesting to look at, too. Did you know learning could be this exciting?

Baking Soda & Vinegar Bubbly Painting

I'm guessing you've probably mixed baking soda and vinegar before. It makes a fun bubbly reaction! But have you ever painted with it? In this fun painting project, you'll make art that actually bubbles and foams before your eyes as it undergoes a chemical reaction.

When baking soda and vinegar mix, they create an acid-base reaction. The vinegar is the acid and the baking soda is the base. Together they transform into a carbon dioxide gas that's released. This is what makes it bubble!

What You'll Need

several small bowls or cups

baking soda

liquid watercolors or food coloring

paintbrushes

watercolor paper or other thick paper

vinegar

pipettes or eye droppers

trays to contain the mess

Science in Action: *Acid, Base, Carbon Dioxide, Chemical Reactions*

1 Begin by mixing your paint solution. Using a small bowl or cup for each color, mix together baking soda and water to make a spreadable paste. Add a few drops of color to each bowl and mix well. The more color you add, the more vibrant this project will be! It is fun to use primary colors for this project so your colors will mix well.

2 Set your paper in a tray, and, using a paintbrush, paint your paper with the baking soda paint.

3 In another small cup or bowl, pour some white vinegar. Use a pipette or eye dropper to drip it onto the paint on your picture. This is where the magic happens! Let it swirl and mix colors.

4 Try it again to make a new design.

Homemade Exploding Paintballs

This project is messy, but seriously fun to make! These homemade paintballs are worthy of your next backyard party. You'll be creating a chemical reaction in these paintballs between two chemicals: calcium chloride and sodium alginate. Sodium alginate is a polymer (a substance consisting of many molecules) made of seaweed that turns into a gel-like substance when mixed with calcium chloride. When the two combine, the molecules rearrange, causing the alginate to bind with the calcium. These balls will be firm on the outside, but still wet on the inside. When you throw them, they'll pop open and make a splatter of paint.

Science in Action: *Chemical Reaction, Polymer*

1 In a cup, mix together ¾ cups (177 ml) water with 1 tablespoon (15 ml) paint. Repeat this for each color you want to make. Then add 1 teaspoon of sodium alginate to each cup (240 ml) of paint. The mixtures will thicken and get lumpy quickly, so mix as fast as possible. It's okay if there are some lumps. Let the mixtures sit for about two hours. They'll thicken a bit more as they sit.

2 Fill a large pan with water and add 2 tablespoons (30 g) of the calcium chloride powder into the water. Mix until it dissolves. If you have molds, spoon your paint mixture into them. You can do this without molds just as easily, but the molds make for more uniform paintballs. Slide the mold into the large pan of water and let the water cover the whole tray. If you're doing this without molds, just spoon the paint mixture directly into the water.

3 The paint balls will float up slightly. When they have a soft skin on the outside with wet paint on the inside, gently remove them from the water and place them on a plate or tray. They can pop, so be careful.

4 Repeat until you have used up all of your paint mixture.

5 Here's the fun part! Take them outside, where it is okay to get messy. Lay out a large piece of white paper and throw the paintballs at the paper . . . or just throw them at each other! They'll splatter and pop open, spraying paint all over and make amazing colorful art wherever they land!

Cake Baking Experiment

You may not know this, but baking is a science as well as an art. It is a science because reactions happen in the baking process to turn the recipe from just ingredients into the final delicious food. It is an art because you can make such beauty when baking! Each ingredient in a recipe has a part in making the food turn out just right in the end. If you forget to add an ingredient, it will change the final product. For this project you'll experiment with cakes by leaving out ingredients and testing the difference they make in your final cake. Then you get to taste them at the end! What could be better?

Science in Action: *Chemical Reaction, Endothermic Reaction*

1 You'll be making mini cakes four different ways, each time with a slight difference. Use the ingredients list above for the amounts you'll need for each. Beat two eggs in a small bowl. You'll use ⅓ egg for each cake.

Make Cake 1 following the recipe and using all the ingredients.

- For Cake 2, use all ingredients except the oil.
- For Cake 3, use all ingredients except the egg.
- For Cake 4, use all ingredients except the baking powder.

What You'll Need

flour

sugar

salt

milk

vanilla

baking powder

cooking oil

eggs

muffin pans or other small oven safe dishes

masking tape

permanent marker

Cake Ingredients

6 tablespoons (85 g) flour

3 tablespoons (40 g) sugar

1 pinch salt

2 tablespoons (30 ml) milk

¼ teaspoon vanilla

¼ teaspoon baking powder

2 tablespoons (30 ml) cooking oil

⅓ of a beaten egg

THINK ABOUT IT

What does each ingredient do in the cake recipe? Oil gives a chewy texture and adds moisture and flavor to the recipe. Eggs add structure, keeping the cake together and helping it rise. Baking powder also helps the cake rise, giving it a lighter and more airy texture.

2 Spray each cake pan with cooking oil. Label the outside of each pan with the number of the cake, using masking tape and a marker.

3 Bake the cakes in the oven together at 350°F (180°C, or gas mark 4) for about 20 minutes. The edges will be lightly golden and the top will be firm. Remove the cakes from the oven and let cool.

4 Once the cakes are cooled, remove from their pans. Notice the difference in how each one rose.

5 Cut into the cakes and taste each one. Analyze the differences in each cake's texture and taste.

Crystal Flower Garden

Get ready to be wowed by these beautiful crystal flowers! How does this process work? The liquid of the crystal solution soaks into the cotton swabs using capillary action. The ammonia in the solution speeds up the process of evaporation, leaving behind the salt and bluing mixture which form the crystals! Adding color is just to make them even more amazing.

Science in Action: *Capillary Action, Chemistry, Evaporation*

What You'll Need

sponge

scissors

cotton swabs

small glass bowl

liquid watercolor or other coloring

protective gloves

safety goggles

apron or other protective clothing

small bowl

salt

liquid bluing

ammonia

craft stick

1 Cut a sponge to fit the bottom of the small glass bowl. Make 5–7 small cuts in the sponge, then slip the cotton swabs into the holes in the sponge. Place the sponge in your glass bowl.

2 Using your liquid coloring, saturate the tips of the cotton swabs with color. Let the color drip down the side and on the bottom of the sponge to give more color as the crystals grow up to the tips.

3 In a small bowl, mix your crystal solution. Combine 3 tablespoons (45 ml) salt, 3 tablespoons (45 ml) bluing, and 2 tablespoons (30 ml) ammonia. Stir with a craft stick until salt is mostly dissolved.

4 Spoon the crystal solution over the top of the cotton swabs. Make sure to get it on the top tips of the cotton swabs in addition to the sponge if you want growth there too.

5 Let sit untouched for up to a week. You'll see changes and growth each day. These crystals are very fragile and soft to the touch. They'll crumble with any movement, so be careful.

Safety Note
This project requires adult supervision. The chemical reaction involves some strong chemicals, so an adult should help. Always take precautions: Wear protective gloves, goggles, and clothing, and work in a well-ventilated area.

Growth of crystals

After 1 day

After 3 days

After 6 days

Color Mixing Bath Bombs

Bath bombs are so much fun to use in the tub! Learn how to make your own but add a fun color mixing aspect to it too! The fizziness of a bath bomb is caused when the citric acid and the baking soda interact with the water in the bath. The reactions create carbon dioxide gas, which makes bubbles. The bubbles pop and release the smell! Adding cornstarch to the mixture slows down the reaction, helping the bath bomb last longer in the tub. What colors can you create?

Science in Action: *Carbon Dioxide, Chemical Reaction, Chemistry*

What You'll Need

1 cup (220 g) baking soda

½ cup (65 g) cornstarch

½ cup (35 g) citric acid

½ cup (120 g) Epsom salt

2 tablespoons (30 ml) melted coconut oil

1 tablespoon (15 ml) water

12–15 drops essential oil or other scent

bath safe coloring

bath bomb molds

mixing bowl

1 Mix together baking soda, cornstarch, citric acid, and Epsom salt in a mixing bowl. Add water and oil and mix until the mixture is crumbly and you can press and squeeze it together into a ball. If you're using only one scent, you can add it now. If you want multiple scents, wait until the next step.

2 Divide the mixture into multiple bowls to make different colors. Mix in 12–20 drops of color depending on how vibrant you want the colors to be. Mix well.

3 Press mixture into the bath bomb molds. To make bath bombs of multiple colors, do each half of the sphere a different color that mixes well together, such as red and yellow. To make rainbow layered bath bombs, layer each color one at a time in the mold. Press until you fill the molds all the way full, and they are slightly rounded. Press the two halves together tightly. Let dry for 24 hours.

4 Carefully remove from molds by tapping the outside to loosen them.

5 Use as desired in the bathtub or play with them in a plastic tub.

Making Plastic from Milk

It may sound crazy, but it's true. You can indeed make plastic out of milk! Molecules of casein, the protein in milk, form a chain called a polymer. There are many kinds of polymers. Plastics are made out of polymers because they can be molded and formed into shapes. In this experiment you can make your own molded plastic shapes from just two ingredients. This type of plastic made from casein was once used to make all kinds of things, including buttons, jewelry, ornaments, and pens.

Science in Action: *Casein, Molecules, Polymer*

What You'll Need

2 cups (480 ml) milk

3 teaspoons (15 ml) white vinegar

slotted spoon

paper towels

stove or microwave

pot or bowl

mixing spoon

molds or cookie cutters

coloring (optional)

1 Heat the milk on the stove or in a microwave until hot, but not boiling. Remove from heat and add the white vinegar and stir well. The milk will curdle and separate once the vinegar is added. The thick white part is the casein or milk protein.

2 Scoop the casein out of the liquid and dry it out on a paper towel.

3 If you want to add coloring, do it now. Press the bits of casein into molds or cut and shape as desired. Try making something usable such as beads, key chains, or buttons, or just make little toys.

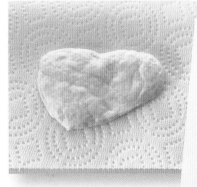

4 Allow the shapes to dry for about 2 days.

5 Once hardened, the plastic can also be painted with acrylic paints if desired.

Magic Color-Changing Lemonade

Red cabbage juice is a natural pH indicator because it contains a substance called *anthocyanin*. When you mix anthocyanin with another substance, it changes colors to indicate whether that substance is an acid or base. In this experiment, you use cabbage to make a color-changing lemonade. Because lemon juice is an acid, it turns a bright pink color when the cabbage juice is added. Drinking cabbage juice may sound gross, but once it's mixed with lemonade, it's barely noticeable! It still tastes delicious.

Science in Action: *Acid, Base, pH Indicator*

What You'll Need

red cabbage, half head

cooking pot

strainer

large bowl

½ cup (64 g) sugar

ice cube trays

freezer

pitcher

large spoon

frozen lemonade concentrate (or make it fresh)

drinking glasses

1 Begin by cutting up a half head of red cabbage into small pieces. Put your cabbage into a large cooking pot and cover with water. Bring to a boil and cook until the cabbage loses most of its color and the water turns dark blue. Remove from heat and allow it to cool completely.

2 Strain the cabbage from the water, pouring the liquid into a separate bowl. To sweeten it a touch, add the sugar to the cabbage water. Pour the cabbage water into ice cube trays and freeze overnight.

3 Make the lemonade. We used frozen lemonade concentrate, but you can make it from lemons, water, and sugar. For this project to work, the mixture just needs to have real lemon juice in it.

Safety Note
This project may require adult supervision. Kids who don't have experience working in the kitchen or using a knife should ask an adult for help, especially when cutting the cabbage.

4 Pour the lemonade into your glass and add a few cabbage juice ice cubes.

5 Watch the color change as the ice melts!

Oil & Water Painting

If you've ever tried to mix oil and water, you'll see that they separate quickly and won't combine. Oil and water are *immiscible*, meaning they won't combine because water molecules have a positive side and a negative side, but oil molecules are evenly balanced. When you try mixing them, the water and oil molecules are more attracted to themselves than to each other. In this art project, you'll use these properties to your advantage. Turns out a little oil, water, and paint will make a beautiful work of art!

What You'll Need

bin or tub

water

eye dropper

cooking oil

watercolor paper

liquid food coloring

tray

Science in Action: *Immiscible, Molecules, Polarity*

1 Fill a bin or tub with water. Use an eye dropper to drop oil into the water. Try making oil drops of varying sizes. The oil will sit on top of the water.

2 Float the paper on the water and press it down through the water. Remove the paper and place it on a tray. There will be oil spots all over the paper.

3 Place the paper on a tray and use an eye dropper to drip colors onto your paper. You can use liquid watercolors or regular watercolor paints. The color will resist the oil spots and make beautiful art!

4 Try mixing colors to see what you can create.

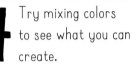

5 When your paintings are dry, cut them into smaller sizes and make cards for friends!

TRY THIS!

Rubbing Alcohol & Watercolor Painting

This painting technique also creates beautiful, unexpected art. Watercolor paints have chemicals in them that bind the pigments to the paper. But when rubbing alcohol is added to the paper, the paint pigments and the alcohol can't mix, so the paint repels, leaving white spots on the paintings.

Color & Light

You may not have considered color to be a part of science, but it is! In this chapter we'll look at how color and light work together in so many ways to inspire scientists and artists alike.

Sometimes what we see with our eyes is not always what it seems. Learn how light and color can be separated to create more colors, why color mixing is a science, and even how the sun can create art. Have fun exploring and creating!

Glowing Highlighter Art

Did you know that highlighter markers glow under a blacklight? In this fun and easy art project, you can create glowing artwork just by using highlighters! Highlighter markers contain fluorescent chemicals that react to ultraviolet light. They absorb and convert light energy, allowing your eyes to see the colors more intensely. When you shine a black light on the fluorescent colors, they appear to glow!

Science in Action: *Color Spectrum, Fluorescent*

What You'll Need

highlighter markers in several colors

black and white paper

black light flashlight or light bulb

1 Draw some designs and scenes on both black and white pieces of paper, using different colors of highlighter markers.

2 We drew planets and constellations, but you can draw whatever you'd like! You'll notice that some colors glow better than others.

3 Take it to another level by removing the ink tube from the highlighter and squeezing out the ink to get a splattered look. This gets messier, but it's so much fun! Now turn on the blacklight. You can use a blacklight flashlight or get a blacklight bulb and replace the regular bulb in any light or lamp.

Solar Prints

Solar printing, also called *cyanotype*, is a process of printing that originated in the 1800s as an early form of photography. Sir John Herschel (1792–1871) invented the process and used it to recreate his notes. In 1843, a botanist named Anna Atkins (1799–1871) used cyanotype to create an album of algae. She is considered to be the first female photographer. You've probably heard of blueprints? The cyanotype process was how blueprints were originally made, giving them their name.

Cyanotypes are made by mixing two different chemicals: ammonium ferric citrate and potassium ferricyanide. When these two chemicals are mixed together, they have a yellowish-green color, but when exposed to UV light, a chemical reaction causes it to turn a bright blue. If you place an object on a paper that's coated with the cyanotype mixture and set it out in the sun, it will leave a print of the object, kind of like a photograph! Make your own cyanotype images in this amazing project.

Science in Action: *Chemistry, Photosensitive, Solutions*

What You'll Need

- plastic or latex gloves
- safety goggles
- cyanotype chemical set (includes ammonium ferric citrate and potassium ferricyanide)
- small bowl
- craft stick for mixing
- paintbrush
- white watercolor paper, cardstock, or fabric
- various objects for printing
- dish bin
- towel

1 On a day when the sun is shining, mix the two chemicals. You can buy a ready-made cyanotype set or purchase the two chemicals individually. In a small bowl, mix equal parts ammonium ferric citrate with potassium ferricyanide. Once the chemicals are combined, the mixture must be used within 4 hours, so only mix as much as you'll need.

2 Working in a dark place, use a paintbrush to brush the solution onto some thick paper or fabric. Allow the mixture to dry completely in the dark. It will take a few hours. The paper or fabric will be a greenish color. Store any unused chemicals in a dark container.

3 Plan out designs for the solar prints, placing the objects in a pattern on the paper or fabric.

4 Place the paper or fabric in the sunlight or another UV light for at least 30 minutes.

5 Take the objects off your paper and remove the paper from the light source. The prints will look sort of golden colored at this point with the design darker and the surrounding area lighter colored. Immediately move to the next step. If you can't rinse them immediately, put the papers in a dark place until you can.

6 Set your prints in a dish bin filled with cool water and submerge them for about five minutes. You'll see the colors change as you rinse them. Move the papers or fabric to a towel to dry.

7 Your finished pictures will be a vibrant blue. You can make beautiful prints that are worthy of framing with this cyanotype process!

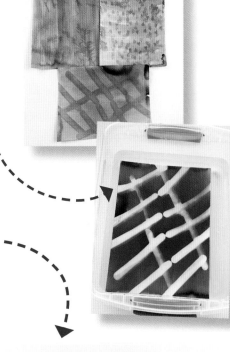

Safety Note
This project requires adult supervision. Everyone should wear plastic or latex gloves and safety goggles while handling the cyanotype chemicals.

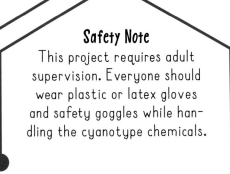

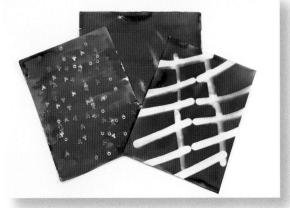

Radial Chromatography

Chromatography is a technique in science that is used to separate a mixture to see what it's made of. The mixture is dissolved in a liquid and filtered out using a medium, such as a filter paper. This activity involves testing out different black markers to see what pigments are included in the ink mixture. You may be surprised by the results!

Science in Action: *Absorption, Chromatography, Mixtures, Pigments*

What You'll Need

2 small bowls or cups

rubbing alcohol

various types of black markers and pens

filter paper (can also use coffee filters or paper towels)

small tray

eye dropper

1 In one of the small bowls, place a small amount of water; in the other, pour a small amount of rubbing alcohol. With a variety of different markers, draw some designs in the center of the filter paper. Try a few different types of markers for different results. We used permanent black markers, washable black markers, black pens, and wet-erase markers. You can mix them, using two different types of markers on one paper, or keep them separate.

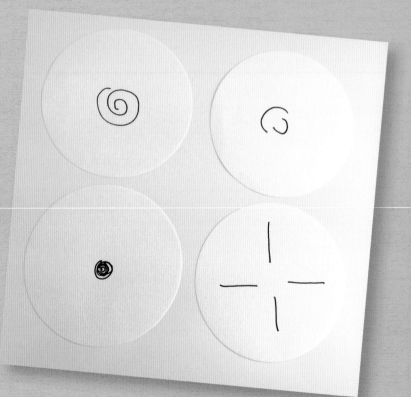

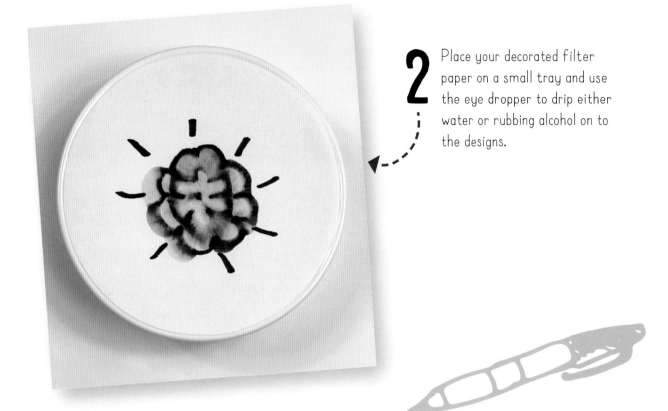

2 Place your decorated filter paper on a small tray and use the eye dropper to drip either water or rubbing alcohol on to the designs.

3 Test out both water and rubbing alcohol with each type of marker to see which one reacts with the ink and causes it to separate. (Hint: Permanent markers react better with the rubbing alcohol.)

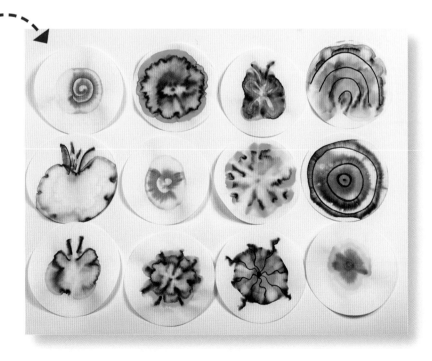

4 Which markers produced the most colors?

X-ray Nature Art

Have you ever broken a bone and needed to have an X-ray done?
An X-ray is a procedure that takes pictures of the inside of
your body. Doctors use them to help diagnose medical problems.

While this project is called an X-ray, it's really just made to look
like one. For this project, you'll use leaves, flowers, or even insects
to create beautiful nature prints that look like X-ray images!

The fun part is seeing how the paint resists the areas where
crayon is applied, leaving only the images of the leaves behind.
Water and wax don't mix—they actually resist one another
instead!

Science in Action: Anatomy, Biology, Botany

What You'll Need

leaves, flowers, or other natural objects that are mostly flat

scissors

contact paper

white paper

crayons

black tempera paint, watered down

paper cup

foam brush or larger paintbrush

1 Collect some objects from nature.
You can use leaves, flowers,
feathers, butterfly wings, or
anything that's mostly flat. Cut
a piece of contact paper and peel
off half of the paper from it.
Place your objects on the exposed
sticky side. Peel the other half of
the paper and fold it over, sealing
your objects inside.

3 Water down some black tempera paint in a paper cup and use a paintbrush or foam brush to paint over the crayon rubbings.

2 Lay a piece of white paper over the top of the contact paper and rub over it with the side of a peeled crayon. If you use white crayons they will look more like X-rays, but colored crayons are easier to see and turn out great, too! Rub over the contact paper a few times to get the imprint of all of the shapes.

4 Let the paint dry, then hold your images up to the light or to a window to see your X-rays.

Shadow Drawings

When sunlight reaches an object that is not see through, the object casts a shadow. A shadow is the absence of light. As the Earth rotates around the sun throughout the day, the shadows move and change size. Watch the shadows to see when a good time of day might be to do this activity. Different objects can make some amazing-shaped shadows. Find some fun things to set up and trace the shadows to create this artwork!

Science in Action: *Earth Rotation, Shadows*

What You'll Need

small table or desk

plants or other objects to draw

string

scissors

jar (optional)

pencil

paper

markers or paints

paintbrush (optional)

1 Choose a sunny spot to set up your drawing. You can do this outside, or next to a sunny window. Set up your table so the sun is shining onto it, casting shadows onto your table. You may have to watch the sunlight for a day to see what time is best to catch the sun as it shines through the window if doing this inside. You may also notice that the shadows may move even as you're drawing, so try to catch them quickly!

2 Lay out some paper on a table or desk. Find some items to draw such as flowers, leaves, branches, or even some small toys.

3 Tie the items you're drawing onto a string and hang them up in your sunny window. If you're outside, set the flowers or branches in a jar on the end of the table closest to the sun.

4 Use pencils or other art supplies to trace the shadows from your objects. Color or paint them as much as you like after drawing.

TRY THIS!

Prism Drawing

In 1665, scientist Isaac Newton (1643–1727) allowed a beam of light to shine through a glass prism. Try making your own rainbows with glass prisms. Set up your prisms in a dark place with a piece of paper underneath. Shine a flashlight through the prisms in various directions until you find rainbows or light patterns that you like. Use crayons or colored pencils to draw the patterns you see. You may want another set of hands to hold the light while you draw.

Nebula Paintings

A *nebula* is a cloud or fog of dust and gases in space. Nebulae (plural of nebula) are hundreds of light years in diameter. They're bright and colorful because of the stars in and around them. Some nebulae even form stars and planets over time. There are many breathtaking pictures taken by scientists that you can find online. Find some that you like and recreate them in your own way!

Science in Action: *Astronomy, Nebula, Space*

What You'll Need

pictures of nebulae or galaxies

acrylic paints in white plus a variety of colors

black poster or cardstock

sponge

paintbrush

foam brush

1 Find a few nebulae online and study them for ideas for how to create your painting. Begin creating your nebula by applying paint to the black poster board. You can use a variety of painting techniques and brushes to get different textures in these paintings. Use a sponge to blot splotches of color around your paper.

2 Or create designs and different bodies of stars and galaxies simply by dabbing paint with a regular paintbrush. A foam brush is useful for blending and softening some of the colors.

3 Spatter white paint over the nebula to create the look of stars.

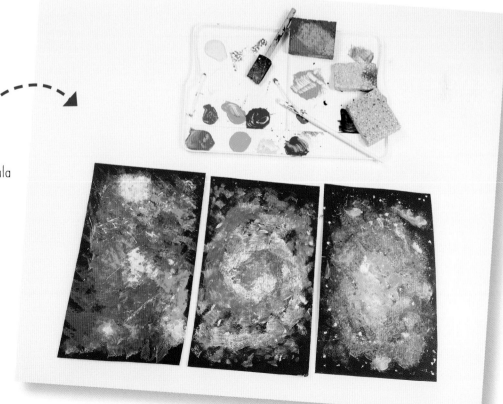

Seurat Pointillism

A French artist named Georges Seurat (1859–1891) is well known for creating a new style of painting called *Pointillism*, which uses small dots or strokes of different colors. He didn't mix or blend the colors, but when you look at his paintings from a distance, it looks as if the colors are blended. The term Pointillism refers to making the dots. This style of painting is also known as *Divisionism* or *Chromoluminarism*. Our eyes are amazing organs! Even though the Pointillism style of painting doesn't mix colors, our eyes do it for us! In fact, this style of painting can make the colors appear more vibrant to our eyes.

What You'll Need

copies of paintings by Georges Seurat

thick white paper

pencil

cotton swabs

tempera paint

Science in Action: *Anatomy, Color*

1 Choose a Seurat painting you want to use as your guide or come up with your own idea of something to draw and paint. Sketch out your drawing with a pencil.

2 Using cotton swabs, paint your picture. Use only dots of different colors to make the colors in your image blend.

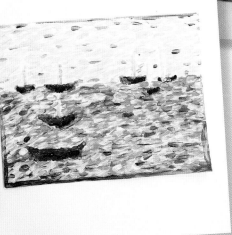

3 Continue dotting until you've finished your artwork. It will take some time and patience, but it's worth it.

TRY THIS! If you look at the painting from up close, you'll see all of the dots, but as you step back from it, colors blend, revealing the images in the paintings that are meant to be seen.

Marbled Paper

Marbled paper is an art technique that has been used for over a thousand years in several countries, including Japan, Turkey, and China. There's some interesting science behind it, too! This project uses shaving cream, and the soap in the shaving cream reacts to the water in the coloring you use. Soap is *amphipathic*, meaning it has molecules that repel water on one end and attract water on the other end. When you drip the coloring onto the shaving cream, it rests on top because it only interacts with the side of the soap molecules that are attracted to water.

Science in Action: *Amphipathic, Hydrophilic, Hydrophobic, Molecules*

What You'll Need

large tray

foam shaving cream

food coloring or liquid watercolors

toothpick

thick pieces of paper

spatula

1 Fill your tray with shaving cream. Spread it around the tray evenly. Drip your coloring onto the top of the shaving cream. Use any color combination you would like. The coloring will sit on top of the shaving cream.

2 Use a toothpick to swirl the colors around to look like marbling.

3 Press your paper onto the top of the shaving cream and coloring.

4 Pull up the paper and hold it over a sink, using a spatula to scrape off the shaving cream.

5 Let the paper dry and try it again with a new piece of paper and different colors!

Homemade Kaleidoscope

A kaleidoscope is a fun toy that you've probably played with before. Making your own is easy and exciting! This is the perfect example of combining art and science because the images you can create in a kaleidoscope are so beautiful! They work by reflecting light from the end of the scope. The multiple mirrors reflect the objects as well as each other, creating amazing colorful patterns that always look different.

Science in Action: *Color, Reflection*

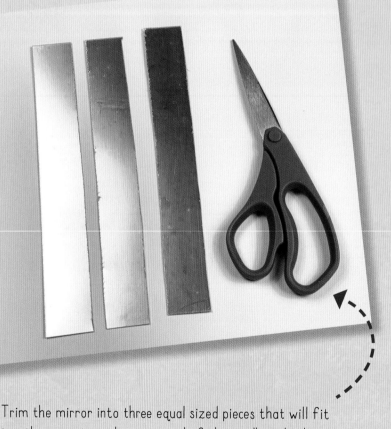

What You'll Need

flexible plastic adhesive mirror

cardboard tube from a paper towel roll

clear tape

hot glue gun

scissors

craft foam or card-stock paper

hole punch

wax paper

2 plastic food lids, small enough to fit inside cardboard tube

colored transparent beads

sequins

decorative paper (optional)

markers or paints

1 Trim the mirror into three equal sized pieces that will fit together as a triangle at one end of the cardboard tube. In a standard paper towel tube, we cut the mirrors to 1¼ x 8" (3 x 20.5 cm).

2 Assemble the triangle and secure on backside with tape. Slide the mirror into the end of the cardboard tube. Add a few dabs of hot glue on each side of the mirror to keep it in place.

3 Cut a circle large enough to cover one end of the cardboard tube from cardstock paper or craft foam. Use a hole punch to cut a hole in the center of the circle, then cut it to about ½" (1 cm) in diameter. Hot-glue the circle to the end of the cardboard tube to make the viewing hole.

4 Cut a piece of wax paper to cover one of the plastic lids and glue it onto the outside. Put the glue just around the rim of the lid so you won't see it through the kaleidoscope. This will allow light to pass through the kaleidoscope but make it slightly frosted. Having it not completely clear keeps the focus on the objects inside of the kaleidoscope instead of seeing what is beyond it.

5 Fill the other plastic lid with beads and sequins. Add a variety of colors and shapes to make the view through the kaleidoscope extra colorful! You could also add small pieces of colored tissue paper or confetti.

6 Glue or tape the two lids together to tightly secure them. We used a layer of hot glue along the edges to secure the two lids together and then added a layer of tape around the outer edge.

7 Glue the clear side of the lids to the end of the cardboard tube by hot gluing around the edge of the tube.

8 Decorate the outside of the cardboard tube however you like with colored paper, paint, or stickers.

9 Look through the viewing hole and turn your kaleidoscope to see all the beautiful shapes and colors!

Acknowledgments

Thank you to my family who once again put up with my long hours of testing and re-testing ideas and projects for my second book! You put up with extra mess, and fewer home-cooked meals. Writing a book is a sacrifice for the whole family, and I know you'll all be glad when the process is over. I love you all for helping me achieve my dreams.

Thanks to my blog supporters and followers over at Teach Beside Me. Your kind words, small purchases, and regular visits to my site help keep me going.

Thanks to my mom, who always gives the best support and ideas! You are amazing.

Thanks to my dad, who gave me his love of science. You taught me so many things over the years about the birds we saw through our windows and the way car engines work.

To my grandpa, Pops. While you may not be here on earth anymore, I will always remember you and your big dreams. Your inquisitive mind and constant love of inventing new things was passed on to me. I will never forget helping you build the parts for your inventions.

Thank you to my amazing publishing team! I love working with you and am honored to be invited back for a second book.

To all of my science teachers over the years who inspired me to love science and see the beauty of it. And to all teachers currently teaching science, thank you. You are doing such an amazing thing. Keep inspiring your students by sharing your passion with them.

About the Author

KARYN TRIPP is a former public school teacher turned homeschool mom of four kids. Through her online community, TeachBesideMe.com, she shares with teachers and homeschool parents how to make learning enjoyable and engaging, and eases the burdens of her fellow educators by offering exciting and memorable learning activities. Karyn is also a member of STEAM Kids Books, a group of educational bloggers—engineers, teachers, math nerds, art lovers, and writers—who have thus far co-written and self-published three titles. She lives in Cedar Hills, Utah.

Index

Absorption, 8, 94–95
Acid, 8, 72–73, 84–85
Aerodynamic, 8, 38–39
Amphipathic, 8, 104–105
Anatomy, 8, 96–97, 102–103
Animation, 8, 34–35
Anthocyanin, 84
Aquaponics, 8, 58–59
Astronomy, 8, 100–101
Atoms, 8, 54–55
Automaton, 24–27

Baking soda, projects using, 72–73, 80–81
Base, 8, 72–73, 84–85
Bath Bombs, Color Mixing, 80–81
Beads, projects using, 48–49, 54–55, 106–109
Biology, 8, 52, 56–57, 58–59, 96–97
Botany, 8, 60–63, 64–65, 96–97
Buttons, 28–29

Cajal, Santiago Ramón, 66
Cake Baking Experiment, 76–77
Calcium chloride, 74
Cams, 8, 24–27
Capillary action, 8, 78–79
Carbon dioxide, 9, 72–73, 80–81
Cardboard box, for Spin Art Machine, 16–17
Cardboard, projects using, 24–27, 28–29, 30–33, 36–37
Cardboard tube, for Homemade Kaleidoscope, 106–109
Cardstock, projects using, 20–21, 92–93, 100–101, 106–107
Casein, 9, 82–83
Cells, 9, 66–67
Center of gravity/center of mass, 9, 22–23
Centrifugal force, 9, 16–17
Chemical reactions, 9, 72–73, 74–75, 76–77, 80–81
Chemistry, 9, 54–55, 78–79, 80–81, 92–93
Chlorophyll, 9, 56–57
Chromatography, 9, 94–95
Chromoluminarism, 102–103
Circuits, 9, 16–17, 42–43, 48–49
Citric acid, 80–81
Clay, for Balancing Monsters, 22–23

Coin cell battery, projects using, 42–43, 48–49
Color/color spectrum, 9, 90–91, 102–103, 106–109
Color Mixing Bath Bombs, 80–81
Condensation, 9, 64–65
Conductivity, 9, 42–43
Contact paper, 96–97
Copper tape, for Paper Circuit Cards, 42–43
Cotton swabs, 102–103
Cotton swabs, projects using, 78–79
Craft foam, 30–33, 106–109
Craft foam, projects using, 24–27
Crystal Flower Garden, 78–79
Cyanotype chemical set, for Solar Prints, 92–93

Divisionism, 102–103
DNA, 10, 68
Dominant trait, 10
Dowel (wooden), projects using, 34–35, 48–49
Drag, 10, 38–39

Earth rotation, 10, 98–99
Ecosystem, 10, 64–65
Electricity, 10, 16–17, 42–43, 48–49
Electrons, 10, 54–55
Elements, 10, 54–55
Endothermic reaction, 10, 76–77
Engineering, 10, 16–17
Evaporation, 10, 78–79

Fish Tank, Aquaponic, 58–59
Flashlight, 90–91
Flowers and leaves, 96–97, 98–99
Fluorescent, 10, 90–91
Flying Insect Automation, 24–27
Food coloring, projects using, 72–73, 86–87, 104–105
Food items, projects using, 56–57, 76–77, 84–85
Force, 10, 28–29, 30–33
Fossils, 10
Friction, 10, 30–33

Gear(s), 10, 16–17, 24–27
Google eyes, for Balancing Monsters, 22–23
Gravity, 10, 20–21, 22–23, 38–39

Highlighter markers, 90–91
Hobby motor, for Spin Art Machine, 16–17
Hydrophilic, 10, 104–105
Hydrophobic, 10, 104–105

Immiscible, 10, 86–87

Kaleidoscope, Homemade, 106–109
Kinetic energy, 10, 14, 18–19, 46–47

Laws of motion (Newton), 11, 20–21, 28–29
Leaves and flowers, 96–97, 98–99
LED lights, projects using, 42–43, 48–49
Lemonade, Magic Color-Changing, 84–85
Levers, 11, 36–37
Lift, 11, 38–39
Light-up cards, 42–43
Light-Up Pipe Cleaner Shapes, 48–49
Liquid watercolors. See Watercolor paints, projects using

Machines, 11, 24–27
Magnetism, 11, 46–47, 50–51
Marbled Paper, 104–105
Marbles, for Aquaponic Fish Tank, 58–59
Mechanical energy, 11, 24–27
Metal brads, projects using, 30–33, 36–37, 68–69
Milk, Making Plastic from, 82–83
Mirror (plastic), for Homemade Kaleidoscope, 106–109
Mixture(s), 11, 94–95
Mobile, Atom Model, 54–55
Molecules, 11, 54–55, 82–83, 86–87, 104–105
Monkey Climbing Toy, 30–33

Nebula, 11
Nebula Paintings, 100–101
Necklaces, Tiny Terrarium, 64–65
Nervous system, 11, 66–67
Neuron Blow Paintings, 66–67
Neurons, 11, 66–67
Neutrons, 11, 54–55
Newton, Isaac, 20, 99
Nucleus, 54

Paintballs, Homemade Exploding, 74–75
Paintings
  Baking Soda & Vinegar Bubbly Painting, 72–73
  Nebula Paintings, 100–101
  Neuron Blow, 66–67
  Oil & Water Painting, 86–87
  Seurat Pointillism, 102–103
Paints, Homemade Natural, 56–57
Paints, projects involving, 74–75, 96–97, 100–101. See also Watercolor paints, projects using
Paleontology, 11
Paper Airplane Physics, 38–39
Paper cup, projects using, 34–35, 48–49, 96–97
Pebbles, 58–59
Pendulum, 11, 46–47
Persistence of vision, 11, 34–35
PH indicator, 11, 84–85
Photosensitive, 11, 92–93
Photosynthesis, 12, 56–57
Physics, 12, 14, 16–17
Pigments, 12, 56–57, 94–95
Pipe cleaners, projects using, 24–27, 30–33, 48–49, 54–55
Plant pigments, 56
Plants, projects involving, 64–65, 96–97, 98–99
Plastic cup, projects using, 18–19, 24–27
Pointillism, 102–103
Polarity, 12, 50–51, 86–87
Polymer, 12, 74–75, 82–83
Pom poms, for Balancing Monsters, 22–23
Potential energy, 12, 14, 18, 46–47
Prism drawing, 99
Protons, 12, 54–55
Punnett, Reginald, 68
Punnett Square, 12, 68–69

Recessive trait, 12, 68–69
Recycling, 12, 60–63
Reflection, 12, 106–109
Rotary movement, 24–27
Rubber band(s), projects using, 18–19, 30–33

Scientific concepts, definitions of, 8–13
Seeds (plant), 58–59, 60–63
Sequins, for Homemade Kaleidoscope, 106–109
Seurat, Georges, 102–103
Shadows, 12, 98–99
Shaving cream, for Marbled Paper, 104–105
Simple machines, 12, 36–37
Skewers (wooden), projects using, 22–23, 24–27, 28–29
Sodium alginate powder, for Homemade Exploding Paintballs, 74–75
Solar Prints, 92–93
Solution(s), 12, 92–93
Sound Wave Art, 44–45
Sound waves, 12, 44–45
Space, 13, 100–101
Spin Art Machine, 16–17
Spinner, Rainbow Gravity, 20–21
Spinning Helicopter Toy, 18–19
Spinning Top Games, 28–29
Straw(s), projects using, 18–19, 20–21, 24–27, 66–67
Supplies, list of, 6–7

Technology, 13, 44–45
Terrariums, Tiny, 64–65
Thrust, 13, 38–39
Toothpick(s), projects using, 18–19, 30–33, 104–105
Torque, 13, 28–29
Transpiration, 13, 64–65

Vials (glass), for Tiny Terrariums, 64–65
Vinegar, projects using, 72–73, 82–83

Watercolor paints, projects using, 66–67, 72–73, 78–79, 87, 104–105
Wavelengths, 13, 44–45
Wheat seeds, for Aquaponic Fish Tank, 58–59
Wire, for Atom Model Mobile, 54–55

X-Ray Nature Art, 96–97

Yogurt cup, for Aquaponic Fish Tank, 58–59

Zoetrope, Paper Cup, 34–35

To my family, the people who inspired me to start it all!

Brimming with creative inspiration, how-to projects, and useful information to enrich your everyday life, Quarto Knows is a favorite destination for those pursuing their interests and passions. Visit our site and dig deeper with our books into your area of interest: Quarto Creates, Quarto Cooks, Quarto Homes, Quarto Lives, Quarto Drives, Quarto Explores, Quarto Gifts, or Quarto Kids.

First Published in 2021 by Quarry Books, an imprint of The Quarto Group,
100 Cummings Center, Suite 265-D, Beverly, MA 01915, USA.
T (978) 282-9590 F (978) 283-2742 QuartoKnows.com

Quarry Books titles are also available at discount for retail, wholesale, promotional, and bulk purchase. For details, contact the Special Sales Manager by email at specialsales@quarto.com or by mail at The Quarto Group, Attn: Special Sales Manager, 100 Cummings Center, Suite 265-D, Beverly, MA 01915, USA.

10 9 8 7 6 5 4 3 2 1

ISBN: 978-0-7603-7216-6

Digital edition published in 2021

eISBN: 978-0-7603-7217-3

Library of Congress Cataloging-in-Publication Data is available.

Design and page layout: Laura McFadden Design, Inc.
Photography: Karen Tripp
Illustrations: Adobe and Shutterstock

Printed in China